First published in the United States of America by
Creative Publishing international, Inc., a member of
Quayside Publishing Group, 400 First Avenue North,
Suite 300, Minneapolis, MN 55401.
1-800-328-3895
www.creativepub.com
Visit www.Craftside.Typepad.com for a behind-the-
scenes peek at our crafty world.
ISBN: 978-1-58923-749-0

10 9 8 7 6 5 4 3 2 1

Library of Congress Cataloging-in-Publication
Data available

Guest Designers: Shelby Allaho, Doris Chan, Ellen
Gormley, Sharon Hubert-Valencia, Tatyana Mirer,
and Shannon Mullett-Bowlsby

Technical Editors: K. J. Hay and Karen Manthey

Technical Illustrations: Karen Manthey

Proofreader: Julie Grady

Book Design: Paul Burgess/Burge Agency
Cover Design: Paul Burgess/Burge Agency
Page Layout: Pete Usher + Paul Burgess
Photographs: Shebaguyz Designz;
p126 author photo Christopher Hubert

Printed in China

**Creative Publishing
international**

runway crochet

high-style patterns from top
designers' hooks to yours

margaret hubert

contents

introduction

The craft of crochet has been handed down through generations to daughters and granddaughters, sons and grandsons. Many people still think of crochet as something that their grandmother did and it reminds them of afghans, baby blankets, and layettes; they seldom think of designer fashions.

In the past few years, however, crochet has made a huge impact in the world of women's fashions. At least 25 famous designers from around the world have included crochet fashions in their collections this past year. From movie stars to rock stars, crochet is popping up everywhere. A crocheted granny square dress even made it to the Academy Awards.

It is every designer's dream to watch their creations stroll down the runway, and I am no exception. Rarely are such high style designs available as patterns for crocheters to follow. With this book, I hope to bring that runway experience to you. Runway Crochet is a collection of designs that are on trend, fun to wear, and full of interesting—sometimes challenging—stitch patterns and techniques. I have many designer friends and I asked a few of them to consider designing something "runway worthy" for this book. Their projects are spectacular and the variety of styles and complexity levels assures that there are designs here for everyone.

Included are designs from Shelby Allaho, whose accessories are outstanding and have won prizes in national crochet contests. Doris Chan's flowing skirts are legendary. Ellen Gormley makes lovely shawls and tops. Tatyana Mirer is well known for her expertise in Bruges lace, but she also does wonderful shaping in her crocheted tops. Shannon Mullet–Bowlsby's edgy designs are well known in the crochet world. Sharon Hubert Valencia loves working crochet side to side, and always tries to come up with a new and challenging way to do this. I have often wondered what has made this explosion of crochet popularity happen. I design both knit and crochet projects, but in the last several years, my crochet patterns have been far more sought out than my knitting patterns. I think one of the reasons for this phenomenon is the abundance of gorgeous yarns in every imaginable natural fiber—silk, cashmere, cotton, fine merino wool, bamboo, even corn. These yarns lend themselves to the lovely texture of crochet stitches; they drape beautifully and flatter every body type. The Internet has made it possible for crocheters everywhere to have access to all of this fabulous yarn.

Another reason for crochet's popularity is that a fashionable crocheted garment makes a woman feel great. I recently crocheted a lacy scarf as a gift for a friend in a nursing home. When I went to visit on a summer day, she was wearing the scarf. I asked if she was cold, and she said "No, it just makes me feel so pretty."

That says it all, women love to feel pretty!

So get those hooks out, choose one of the beautiful patterns in the book, and crochet yourself a spectacular garment or accessory.

Margaret

I would like to dedicate this book to all of my wonderful family for their constant support.

sweaters and jackets

Skill Level

Experienced

Yarn

Art yarn Rhapsody Light Silver Glitter; 50% silk, 50% kid mohair with Lurex; 400 yd (366 m)/2.8 oz (80 g); #286: 3 (4, 4) skeins

juliet jacket

The Juliette Jacket was inspired by my love of Shakespeare and Elizabethan times. The lovely gowns, with their ornate embroidery and incredible details, have always intrigued me. When I first saw this gorgeous silk and mohair yarn, light as a feather, with a hint of glitter, I immediately pictured a lovely, very elegant jacket and started sketching my idea. This jacket is a challenge, but worth the effort.

Designed by Margaret Hubert

Hooks
4/E (3.5 mm)
5/F (3.75 mm)
6/G (4 mm)
8/H (5 mm)

Gauge
With 4/E hook, 6 ch-3 spaces and 10 rows in Body pattern = 4" (10 cm)

Notions
Yarn needle
Three ½" (13 mm) buttons
Stitch markers

Finished Sizes
Women's sizes S (M, L)
Finished Bust: 35 (39, 43)" (89 [99, 109] cm)
Finished Length: 19 (20, 21)" (48.5 [51, 53.5] cm)
This is a close fitting garment and does have stretch.

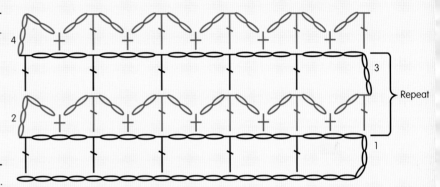

Reduced Sample of Sweater Pattern

Notes
Body of garment is made in one piece from waistline to shoulder, bottom trim is added later. Surprising Shells border is added to sleeve after bottom of sleeve is completed. Surprising Shells border is added to bottom of sweater before button band is put on and before bottom motifs are sewn on. Main body pattern is a multiple of 4 plus 1 sts.

Special Stitches

Shell: *5 dc in same st.*

Reverse sc: *Working from left to right, insert hook in next st to the right, yo, draw yarn through st, yo, draw yarn through 2 loops on hook.*

Body Pattern

Row 1 (RS): *1 dc in 10th ch from hook, *ch 3, skip next 3 ch, 1 dc in next ch; rep from * across, turn.*

Row 2: *Ch 5 (counts as dc, ch 2), *sc in center ch of next ch-3 space, ch 2**, dc in next dc; rep from * across, ending last rep at **, dc in 4th ch of turning ch, turn.*

Row 3: *Ch 6, (counts as dc, ch 3), *dc in next dc, ch 3; rep from * across, dc in the 3rd ch of turn ch, turn.*

Rep Rows 2–3 for pattern.

Body

With 4/E hook, Ch 214 (238, 262).

Row 1 (RS): 1 dc in 10th ch from hook, *ch 3, skip next 3 ch, 1 dc in next ch; rep from * across, turn. (52 [58, 64] ch-3 spaces)

Work even in body pattern until body measures 6 (6½, 7)" from beginning, ending with Row 2 of pattern.

Divide for Back and Fronts
Right Front

Row 1: Work pattern Row 3 until 11 (12, 14) ch-3 spaces are completed, turn.

Row 2: Work pattern Row 2.

Row 3 (decrease row): Ch 3, skip next 2 ch-2 spaces, dc next dc (dec made), *ch 3, dc next dc; rep from * across, turn. (10 [11, 13] ch-3 spaces)

Row 4: Work in pattern Row 2 across to last dc, turn, leaving turning ch un-worked.

Rows 5–6: Work even in pattern.

Rows 7–25: Rep Rows 3–6 (4 times); rep Rows 3–5 once. (5 [6, 8] ch-3 spaces)

Work even in pattern until armhole measures 8½ (9, 9½)" (21.5 [23, 24] cm) from beginning. Fasten off.

Back

Row 1: Skip 8 ch-2 spaces (4 pattern reps) to the left of last st made in Row 1 of right front, join yarn in next dc, ch 6 (counts as dc, ch 3), *dc in next dc, ch 3; rep from * 20 (24, 30) times, dc in next dc, turn, leaving remaining sts unworked. (22 [26, 28] ch-3 spaces)

Work even in pattern as established until back measures same as right front. Fasten off.

Left Front

Row 1: Skip 8 ch-2 spaces (4 pattern reps) to the left of last st made in Row 1 of back, join yarn in next dc, ch 6 (counts as dc, ch 3), *dc in next dc, ch 3; rep from * 9 (10, 12) times, dc in 3rd ch of turning ch, turn. (11 [12, 14] ch-3 spaces)

Row 2: Work pattern Row 2.

Row 3 (decrease row): Work pattern Row 3 across to 2 ch-2 spaces, skip last ch-2, sc, 1 dc in 3rd ch of the beginning ch-5 turn. (10 [11, 13] ch-3 spaces)

Rows 4–6: Work even in pattern.

Rows 7–25: Rep Rows 3–6 (4 times); rep Rows 3–5 once. (5 [6, 8] ch-3 spaces)

Work even in pattern until left front measures same as right front. Fasten off.

Sleeve

(Make 2)

Starting at cuff edge, with 4/E hook, ch 66 (82, 98).

Row 1 (RS): 1 dc in 10th ch from hook, *ch 3, skip next 3 ch, 1 dc in next ch; rep from * across, turn. (15 [19, 23] ch-3 spaces)

Work even in pattern for 6 rows.

Change to 5/F hook, work even in pattern for 6 rows.

Change to 6/G hook, work even in pattern for 5 (7, 9) rows, ending with Row 2 of pattern.

Shape Cap

Row 1: Sl st in first dc, [Sl st across ch 2-space, sc, ch-2 space, dc] twice, ch 6 (counts as dc, ch 3), *dc in next dc, ch 3; rep from * across to within last 2 reps, ending with dc in next dc, turn, leaving last 2 [ch 2-space, sc, ch 2-space, dc] unworked. (11 [15, 19] ch-3 spaces)

Rows 2–7 (9, 11): Work even in pattern for 6 (8, 10) rows.

Next Row (decrease row): Ch 3, skip next ch-3 space, dc in next dc (dec made) continue to work pattern Row 2 across last ch-6 space, skip next 3 ch, dc in next ch (dec made). (9 [13, 17] pattern reps)

Next Row: Ch 3, skip first dc, dc in next dc, work pattern Row 3 across, ending with dc in last dc, turn, leaving turning ch unworked.

Work even in pattern for 5 rows.

Next Row: Change to 4/E hook, work even in pattern Row 3.

Next Row: Ch 1, sc in each ch-2 space across. Fasten off. (18 [26, 34] sc)

Sew underarm sleeve seam.

Bottom Sleeve Border

Rnd 1: Join yarn at underarm seam, ch 1, work 5 sc in each ch-3 space around bottom of sleeve, join with Sl st in first sc. (75 [95, 115] sc)

Rnds 2–5: Ch 1, sc in each sc around, join with Sl st in first sc.

Rnd 6: *Ch 7, skip next 3 sc, sc in next sc; rep from * around, do not join, work in a spiral. Mark beginning of rnd, move marker up as work progresses.

Rnds 7–12: *Ch 7, sc in next ch-7 loop; rep from * around.

Rnd 13: [3 sc, ch 3, 3 sc] in each ch-7 loop around, join with Sl st in first sc. Fasten off.

Surprising Shells Edging

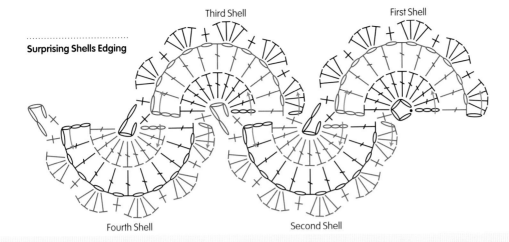

Third Shell First Shell

Fourth Shell Second Shell

Finishing

Mark center top of sleeve cap, match to shoulder seam. Pin sleeve in place and sew in armole. Rep for other seeve.

Surprising Shells Edging

Make a strip with 9 (10, 10) shells for each sleeve (or length needed to fit around sleeve at base of border).

Make a strip with 26 (27, 28) shells for the body (or length needed to fit around bottom edge of body).

Ch 4, join with a Sl st to form a ring.

Row 1: Ch 3 (counts as dc here and throughout), 10 dc in ring, do not join, turn. (11 dc)

Row 2: Ch 4 (counts as dc, ch 1 here and throughout), skip the first dc, *dc in next dc, ch 1; rep from * 8 times, dc in top of turning ch, turn. (11 dc; 10 ch-1 spaces)

Row 3: Ch 1, *4 hdc in next ch-1 space, sc in next ch-1 space; rep from * 4 times, ch 4, 1 sc in 3rd ch of ch-4 turning ch (forming a ring to begin next shell), turn. (shell made)

Row 4: Ch 3, 10 dc in next ch-4 ring, turn. (11 dc)

Row 5: Ch 4, skip first dc, *dc in next dc, ch 1; rep from * 8 times, dc in top of turn-ing ch, do not turn, work sc in the starting ring of the previous motif, turn.

Row 6: Rep Row 3.

Rep Rows 4-6 for shell pattern. At end Row 6 of last shell, omit last ch-4 space, work sc in last ch-1 space, sc in 3rd ch of ch-4 turning ch.

Half Circle Shell Motif

(Make 10)

Note: *Use 5/F hook for S; 6/G hook for M; 8/H hook for L.*

Ch 4, join with a Sl st to form a ring.

Rnd 1 (RS): Ch 1, 8 sc in ring, join with Sl st in first sc. (8 sc)

Rnd 2: Ch 1, 2 sc in each sc around, join with Sl st in first sc. (16 sc)

Work now progresses in rows.

Row 3 (RS): Ch 2, 2 dc in next sc, *dc next sc, 2 dc in next sc; rep from * 3 times (15 dc), turn, leaving remaining sts unworked. (15 dc)

Row 4 (WS): Ch 3 (counts as tr), working in back loops only, sc first st (first mock popcorn made), *(tr, sc) in each dc across, turn. (15 mock popcorns)

Row 5: Ch 3, working in the free loop of Row 3, *2 dc next st, dc next st; rep from * across, turn. (22 dc)

Row 6: Ch 1, working in the back loops only, sc in first st, sc next st, 2 sc in next st, *sc in next 2 sts, 2 sc in next st; rep from * 5 times more, turn, leving turning ch unworked. (28 sc)

Row 7: Ch 1, sc in first sc, sc in each of next 2 sc, 2 sc next sc, *sc in next 3 sc, 2 sc next sc, rep from * across, turn. (35 sc)

Row 8: Ch 1, sc in first sc, *sc next sc, skip next sc, shell in next sc, skip next sc, sc next sc; rep from * 7 times, sc in last sc. Fasten off. (8 shells)

Fill in Flower

(Make 5)

Note: *Use 5/F hook for S; 6/G hook for M; 8/H hook for L.*

Ch 5, join with a Sl st to form a ring.

Rnd 1: Ch 4 (counts as a dc, ch 1), [dc, ch 1] 9 times in ring, join with Sl st in 3rd ch of the beg ch-4.

Rnd 2: *Sc in next ch-1 space, (sc, hdc, trc, hdc, sc) in next ch-1 space; rep from * around, join with Sl st in first sc. Fasten off.

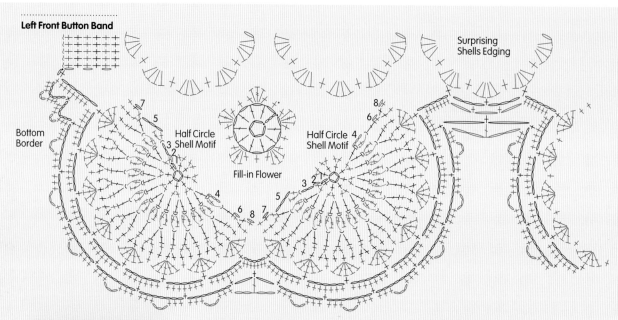

Left Front Button Band

Surprising
Shells Edging

Bottom
Border

Half Circle
Shell Motif

Fill-in Flower

Half Circle
Shell Motif

Before starting button band, sew Surprising Shells borders to body and sleeves following diagram, arranging them as evenly as possible across.

Right Front Buttonhole Band

Before starting button band place pins at half way mark from bottom to beginning of Vee shaping, place pins at each quarter mark.

Row 1: Join yarn at bottom right-hand corner of right front, ch 1, work 44 sc evenly across to beginning of shaping, working 11 sc in each quarter section, turn. (44 sc in all)

Row 2: Ch 1, sc in each sc across, turn.

Row 3: Ch 1, sc in each of the first 3 sc, [ch 3, skip next 2 sc, sc in each of next 9 sc] twice, ch 3, skip 2 sc, sc in each st across, turn. (3 buttonholes made)

Row 4: Ch 1, sc in each sc acros, working 2 sc in each ch-3 space, turn.

Row 5: Ch 1, sc in each sc across, do not turn.

Row 6: Ch 1, reverse sc in each sc across. Fasten off.

Left Front Button Band

Place markers same as on right front edge.

Row 1: With RS facing, join yarn at start of Vee shaping on, left front edge, ch 1, work 44 sc evenly spaced across to bottom left-hand corner, working 11 sc in each quarter section, turn. Remove markers.

Row 2–5: Ch 1, sc in each sc across, turn. Do not turn at end of last row.

Row 6: Ch 1, reverse sc in each sc across. Fasten off.

Neck Border

Start on right front, at Vee shaping, right side facing you.

Row 1: With RS facing, join yarn at beginning of Vee shaping on right front edge, ch 1, work 50 sc evenly spaced across to back neck, work 40 sc across back neck, work 50 sc down left front to beginning of Vee shaping, turn. (140 sc)

Rows 2–4: Ch 1, sc in each sc across, turn.

Row 5: *Ch 7, skip next 4 sc, sc in next sc; rep from * across, turn. (28 ch-7 loops)

Row 6: [3 sc, ch 3, 3 sc] in each ch-7 loop across. Fasten off.

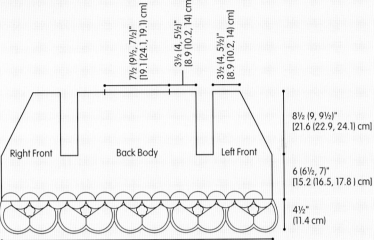

7½ (9½, 7½)" [19.1 (24.1, 19.1) cm]

3½ (4, 5½)" [8.9 (10.2, 14) cm]

3½ (4, 5½)" [8.9 (10.2, 14) cm]

Right Front   Back Body   Left Front

8½ (9, 9½)" [21.6 (22.9, 24.1) cm]

6 (6½, 7)" [15.2 (16.5, 17.8) cm]

4½" (11.4 cm)

34½ (38½, 42½)" [87.6 (97.8, 108) cm]

Finishing

Sew neck border to sides of buttonhole band and button band where they meet at Vee shaping. Sew half circle motifs evenly spaced across bottom of sweater, following diagram for approximate placement. Sew 1 fill-in flower in space between each pair of half circle motifs.

Bottom Border

Note: *Use 5/F hook for S; 6/G hook for M; 8/H hook for L.*

Note: *Placement of 3 sc and 2 ch-3 spaces across bottom edge of edging and between motifs will vary depending on placement of half shell motifs.*

Row 1: With RS facing, join yarn with a Sl st at bottom left-hand corner of left front button band, *[ch 5, sc in center dc of next shell] 17 times, [ch 3, skip approximately 4 sts, sc in edging] twice; rep from * 3 times, [ch 5, sc in center dc of next shell] 16 times, ch 5, Sl st in bottom right-hand corner of right front buttonhole band, turn.

Row 2: Ch 1, sc in first sc, *7 sc in each of the next 17 ch-5 spaces**, [ch 1, sc in next ch-3 space] twice, ch 1; rep from * across, ending last rep at **, sc in last sc, turn.

Row 3: *Ch 7, sc in center sc of next 7-sc group] 8 times [ch 1, sc in center sc of next 7-sc group] twice, [ch 7, sc in center sc of next 7-sc group] 6 times **, ch 1, skip next ch-1 space, sc in next ch-1 space, ch 1, skip next ch-1 space, sc in center sc of next 7-sc group; rep from * across, ending last rep at **, ch 7, sc in center sc of next 7-sc group, ch 7, sc in last sc, turn.

Row 4: Ch 1, (3 sc, ch 3, 3 sc) in each of next 8 ch-7 loops, *ch 2, skip next ch-1 space, dc in next sc, ch 2, skip next ch-1 space, (3 sc, ch 3, 3 sc) in each of next 6 ch-7 loops; rep from * across, (3 sc, ch 3, 3 sc) in each of last 2 ch-7 loops. Fasten off.

Sew buttons to left front opposite buttonholes. Do not block this garment.

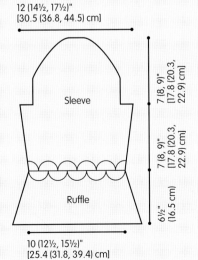

12 (14½, 17½)" [30.5 (36.8, 44.5) cm]

Sleeve

Ruffle

7 (8, 9)" [17.8 (20.3, 22.9) cm]

7 (8, 9)" [17.8 (20.3, 22.9) cm]

6½" (16.5 cm)

10 (12½, 15½)" [25.4 (31.8, 39.4) cm]

Skill Level

Intermediate

Yarn

Berroco Captiva; 60% cotton, 23% polyester, 17% acrylic; 98 yd (90 m)/1.75 oz (50 g), #5515 Laurel: 16 (16, 17, 18) skeins

antonia peplum jacket

Peplum jackets have made a huge appearance in the fashion world, providing a feminine, flattering look that appeals to all ages. After I sketched a design, the search for a suitable yarn began. I wanted a yarn that would convey the romance of the design, yet hold its shape. The soft colors of the ribbon yarn and the crisp way that it worked up seemed just about perfect to me and I love how it turned out.

Designed by
Margaret Hubert

Hooks	Gauge	Notions	Finished Sizes
6/G (4 mm)	1 shell, 1 5 dc rib, 1 shell, 1 5 dc rib = 4", 9 rows = 4"	Yarn needle Stitch markers	Women's sizes S (M, L, XL) Finished bust: 32 (36, 40, 44)" (81.5 [91.5, 101.5, 112] cm)

Reduced Sample
of Pattern

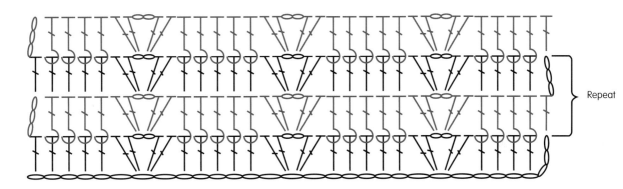

Repeat

Notes

Body is started at waistline, made in one piece to armholes, then divided for fronts and back. Peplum is picked up on the reverse side of the beginning chain, and worked from the waist down.

Special Stitches

Front post double crochet (FPdc): *Yo, insert hook from front to back to front again around the post of next st, yo and draw up loop, [yo and draw through 2 loops on hook] twice.*

Front post double crochet 2 together (FPdc2tog): *Yo, insert hook from front to back to front again around the post of next st, yo and draw up loop, [yo and draw through 2 loops on hook] twice; rep from * once, yo, draw yarn through 3 loops on hook.*

Shell: *(2 dc, ch 2, 2 dc) in same st or space.*

Sc2tog: *[Insert hook in next st, yo, draw yarn through st] twice, yo, draw yarn through 3 loops on hook.*

Body

Ch 127 (143, 159, 175).

Row 1 (RS): Dc in 4th ch from hook, dc in each of next 3 ch, *skip next ch, shell in next ch, skip next ch, dc in each of next 5 ch; rep from * across, turn. (16 [18, 20, 22] groups of dc; 15 [17, 19, 21] shells).

Row 2: Ch 3 (counts as a dc here and throughout), skip first dc, FPdc around the post of each of next 4 dc, *skip next 2 dc of next shell, shell in next ch-2 space, skip next 2 dc of shell, FPdc, around post of each of next 5 dc; rep from * across, ending with FPdc around post of last 4 dc, dc in top of turning ch, turn.

Row 3: Ch 3, 1 dc in each of next 4 FPdc, *skip bext 2 dc, shell in ch-2 space of next shell, skip next 2 dc, dc in each of the next 5 FPdc; rep from * across, turn. Repeat Rows 2–3 for pattern.

Rows 4–18: Work even in pattern, ending with a WS row.

Divide for Back and Fronts

Right Front

Row 19: Ch 3, work in pattern as established until 3 (4, 5, 5) dc-groups and 2 (3, 4, 4) shells are completed, 2 dc in ch-2 space of next shell, turn, leaving remaining sts unworked. (29 [40, 51, 51] sts)

Row 20: Work even in pattern Row 2.

Row 21: Ch 3, work in pattern Row 3 across to last 3 sts, dc2tog, dc in top of turning ch, turn. (28 [39, 50, 50] sts)

Row 22: Ch 3, FPdc2tog in next 2 sts, work in pattern Row 2 across, turn. (27 [38, 49, 49] sts)

Row 23: Ch 3, work in pattern Row 3 across to last 3 sts, dc2tog, dc in top of turning ch, turn. (26 [37, 48, 48] sts)

Rows 24–30: Work even in pattern as established until right front measures 5½ (6, 6½, 7)" (14 [16.5, 18] cm) from beginning, ending with a WS row, turn.

Shape Neck

Row 31: Sl st over first 13 (22, 24, 24) sts, ch 3, work even in pattern across, turn. (13 [15, 24, 24] sts)

Rows 32–36: Work even in pattern as established until armhole measures 7½ (8, 8½, 9)" (19 [20.5, 21.5, 23] cm) from beginning. Fasten off.

Row 22: Ch 3, work in pattern Row 2 across to last 3 sts, FPdc2tog in next 2 sts, dc in top of turning ch, turn. (27 [38, 49, 49] sts)

Row 23: Ch 3, dc2tog, work in pattern Row 3 across, turn. (26 [37, 48, 48] sts)

Rows 24–30: Work even in pattern as established until left front measures 5½ (6, 6½, 7)" (14 [16.5, 18] cm) from beginning, ending with a WS row, turn.

Shape Neck

Row 31: Ch 3, work even in pattern Row 3 across to with last 13 (22, 24, 24) sts, turn, leaving remaining sts unworked. (13 [15, 24, 24] sts)

Rows 32–36: Work even in pattern as established until left front measures same as finished right front. Fasten off.

Peplum

Row 1: With RS facing, working across opposite side of foundation ch, join yarn in first ch, ch 3, 2 dc in next ch, dc in next 2 ch, 2 dc in next ch, *skip next 2 ch, shell in ch at base of next shell, skip next 2 ch, 2 dc in next ch, dc in next 3 ch, 2 dc in next ch; rep from * across, turn. (16 [18, 20, 22] groups of 7 dc, 15 [17, 19, 21] shells)

Rows 2–4: Work even in pattern as established.

Row 5: Work in pattern Row 3, increasing 1 dc at each end of each dc-group. (9 dc in each dc-group)

Rows 6–8: Work even in pattern as established.

Row 9: Work in pattern Row 3, increasing 1 dc at each end of each dc-group. (11 dc in each dc-group)

Rows 10–11: Work even in pattern as established. Fasten off.

Back

Row 19: With RS facing, skip 1 dc-group to left of last st in Row 1 of right front, join yarn in ch-2 space of next shell, ch 3, dc in same space, work even in pattern across until 8 (8, 9, 10) dc-groups and 7 (7, 8, 9) shells are completed, work 2 dc in ch-2 space of next shell, turn, leaving remaining sts unworked. (86 [86, 97, 108] sts)

Row 20: Work even in pattern Row 2.

Row 21: Ch 3, dc2tog, work in pattern Row 3 across to last 3 sts, dc2tog, dc in top of turning ch, turn. (84 [84, 95, 106] sts)

Row 22: Ch 3, FPdc2tog in next 2 sts, work in pattern Row 2 across to last 3 sts, FPdc2tog in next 2 sts, dc in top of turning ch, turn. (82 [82, 93, 104] sts)

Row 23: Ch 3, dc2tog, work in pattern Row 3 across to last 3 sts, dc2tog, dc in top of turning ch, turn. (80 [80, 91, 102] sts)

Rows 24–36: Work even in established pattern until back measures same as finished right front. Fasten off.

Left Front

Row 19: With RS facing, skip 1 dc-group to left of last st in Row 1 of right front, join yarn in ch-2 space of next shell, ch 3, dc in same space, work even in pattern across, turn. (29 [40, 51, 51] sts)

Row 20: Work even in pattern Row 2.

Row 21: Ch 3, dc2tog, work in pattern Row 3 across, turn.

Sleeve

(Make 2)

Note: *Sleeves are made from elbow up to shoulder. Ruffled cuff is added at bottom across foundation ch.*

Ch 51 (55, 59, 63).

Row 1 (RS): Dc in 4th chain from hook (counts as 2 dc), dc in each of the next 5 (7, 9, 11) ch, skip next ch, shell in next ch, skip next ch, *dc in each of the next 5 ch, skip next ch, shell in next ch, skip next ch; rep from * across to last 7 (9, 11, 13) ch sts, dc in each remaining ch across, turn. (49 [53, 57, 61] sts; 6 dc-groups; 5 shells; end groups have 7 [9, 11, 13] dcs; center dc-groups have 5 dcs)

Row 2–8 (8, 10, 10): Work even in pattern as established, ending with a WS row.

Next Row: Ch 3, 2 dc in next FPdc, dc in next 4 (6, 8, 10) FPdc, 2 dc in next st, work in pattern across to last dc-group, 2 dc in next FPdc, dc in next 4 (6, 8, 10) FPdc, 2 dc in next st, dc in top of turning ch, turn. (45 [57, 61, 65] sts; end groups have 9 [11, 12, 15] dcs; center dc-groups have 5 dcs)

Work 9 rows even in pattern as established, ending with a WS row.

2½ (3¾, 4½, 4½)"
[6.4 (9.5, 11.4, 11.4) cm]

10 (9, 10, 9)"
[25.4 (22.9, 25.4, 22.9) cm]

2½ (3, 3, 5)"
[6.4 (7.6, 7.6, 12.7) cm]

2½ (3¾, 4½, 4½)"
[6.4 (9.5, 11.4, 11.4) cm]

Back

Left Front

Right Front

Body

7½ (8, 8½, 9)"
[19.1 (20.3, 21.6, 22.9) cm]

8"
(20.3 cm)

Peplum

5"
(12.7 cm)

Bust: 31 (35, 39, 43)" [78.7 (88.9, 99.1, 109.2) cm]

Bottom of Peplum: 55 (58½, 62, 65½)" [139.7 (148.6, 157.5, 166.4) cm]

Sleeve Cap

Row 1: Sl st over the first 5 (6, 7, 8) sts, ch 3, dc2tog in next 2 sts, dc in each of the next 1 (2, 2, 4) FPdc, work in pattern across to last shell, dc in each of the next 1 (2, 2, 4) FPdc, dc2tog, dc in next dc, turn, leaving remaining sts unworked. (33 [43, 45, 47] sts; end groups have 3 [4, 4, 6] dcs; center dc-groups have 5 dcs)

Row 2–3: Work even in pattern as established.

Row 4: Ch 3, FPdc2tog in next 2 sts, work in pattern Row 2 across to last 3 sts, FPdc2tog in next 2 sts, dc in top of turning ch, turn. (31 [41, 43, 45] sts; end groups have 2 [3, 3, 5] dcs; center dc-groups have 5 dcs)

Row 5–7: Work even in pattern as established.

Row 8: Ch 3, FPdc in the next 1 (2, 3, 4) dc, 2 dc in ch-2 space of next shell, (dec 2 sts made), work in pattern row 2 across to last shell, 2 dc in ch-2 space of last shell, (dec 2 sts made), FPdc in each of the last 1 (2, 3, 4) dc, dc in top of turning ch, turn. (27 [37, 39, 41] sts; end groups have 9 [10, 10, 12] dcs; center dc-groups have 5 dcs)

Row 9: Ch 3, dc2tog, work in pattern Row 3 across to last 3 sts, dc2tog, dc in top of turning ch, turn. (25 [35, 37, 39] sts; end groups have 7 [8, 8, 10] dcs; center dc-groups have 5 dcs)

Row 10: Ch 3, skip next dc, dc in each of the next 0 (1, 1, 3), FPdc around each of the next 5 dc, work in pattern Row 2 across to last 2 (3, 3, 4) sts, dc in each of the next 0 (1, 1, 3) sts, skip next dc, dc in top of turning ch, turn. (23 [33, 35, 37] sts)

Row 11: Work even in pattern Row 3. Fasten off Size S.

Sizes M, L and XL Only

Row 12: Ch 3, dc2tog, work in pattern across to last 3 sts, dc2tog, dc in top of turning ch, turn. Fasten off Size M.

Sizes L and XL Only

Row 13: Work even in pattern Row 3. Fasten off Size L.

Sizes XL Only

Row 14: Ch 3, dc2tog, work in pattern across to last 3 sts, dc2tog, dc in top of turning ch, turn. Fasten off.

Sew sleeve seam.

Ruffled Cuff

Ruffle is worked in rows, leaving a slit on top of sleeve, opposite sleeve seam.

Row 1 (RS): With RS facing, working across opposite side of the foundation ch, join yarn in ch at base of center shell, ch 3, dc in same ch (this adds 2 dc to beg of first dc-group) skip next 2 ch, [2 dc in next ch, dc in each of the next 3 (3, 3, 3) dc, 2 dc in next dc] skip next 2 ch, shell in ch at base of next shell] twice, skip next 2 ch, 2 dc in next ch, dc in each of the next 5 (7, 9, 11), dc, 2 dc in next dc, shell in seam (this forms a new shell), 2 dc in next dc, dc in each of the next 5 (7, 9, 11) dc, 2 dc in next dc, [skip next 2 ch, shell in ch at base of next shell, skip next 2 ch, 2 dc in next ch, dc in next 3 ch, 2 dc in next ch] twice, skip next 2 ch, 2 dc in same ch at base of center shell (this adds 2 dc to last dc-group), turn.

Note: *At the end of last row, there should be 5 shells for each size and the following number of dcs in each group:*

For Small Size: 2 groups of 7 dc; 4 groups of 9 dc.

For Med Size: 2 groups of 7 dc; 2 groups of 9 dc; 2 groups of 11 dc.

For Large Size: 2 groups of 7 dc; 2 groups of 9 dc; 2 groups of 13 dc.

For X Large Size: 2 groups of 7 dc; 2 groups of 9 dc; 2 groups of 15 dc.

Rows 2–4: Work even in pattern as established.

Row 5 (increase row): Work in pattern of Row 3, increasing 1 dc at each end of each dc-group.

Sleeve Trim

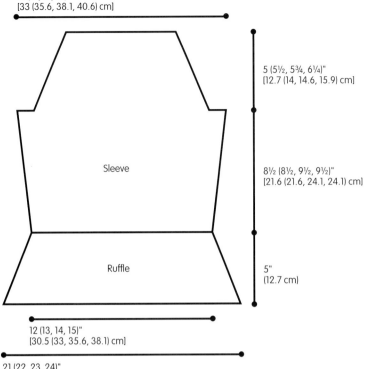

13 (14, 15, 16)"
[33 (35.6, 38.1, 40.6) cm]

5 (5½, 5¾, 6¼)"
[12.7 (14, 14.6, 15.9) cm]

Sleeve

8½ (8½, 9½, 9½)"
[21.6 (21.6, 24.1, 24.1) cm]

Ruffle

5"
(12.7 cm)

12 (13, 14, 15)"
[30.5 (33, 35.6, 38.1) cm]

21 (22, 23, 24)"
[53.3 (55.9, 58.4, 61) cm]

Note: *At the end of last row, there should be 5 shells for each size and the following number of dcs in each group:*

For Small Size: 2 groups of 9 dc; 4 groups of 11 dc.

For Med Size: 2 groups of 9 dc; 2 groups of 11 dc; 2 groups of 13 dc.

For Large Size: 2 groups of 9 dc; 2 groups of 11 dc; 2 groups of 15 dc.

For X Large Size: 2 groups of 9 dc; 2 groups of 11 dc; 2 groups of 17 dc.

Rows 6–8: Work even in pattern as established.

Row 9 (increase row): Work in pattern of Row 3, increasing 1 dc at each end of each dc-group.

Sleeve Trim

Rnd 1: With RS facing, join yarn at bottom of slit, ch 1, sc evenly up side of slit, across last row of cuff, down opposite side of slit, join with Sl st in first sc. Fasten off.

Placket

Before starting placket, divide fronts into 4 quarters by placing markers at the halfway point and then at each quarter.

Row 1: With RS facing, join yarn in bottom right-hand corner of right front, working along right front, work 19 (20, 21, 22) sc evenly spaced in each quarter section of right front, work 3 sc in last sc to turn corner, work 21 (22, 23, 24) sc evenly spaced across to shoulder seam, work 36, (36, 38, 38) sc evenly spaced across back neck edge, work 21 (22, 23, 24) sc evenly spaced across to corner of left front, 3 sc in corner st, work 19 (20, 21, 22) sc evenly spaced in each quarter section of left front to bottom left-hand corner, turn.

Row 2: Ch 1, sc in each sc all across, working 3 sc in center sc of each corner, turn.

Row 3 (buttonhole row): Ch 1, sc in each of the next 23 (24 25, 26) sc, [ch 3, skip next 3 sc, sc in each of the next 9 (10, 11, 12)] 3 times, ch 3, skip next 3 sc (for buttonhole), sc in each sc to top corner of right front, 3 sc in center sc of corner, skip next sc, [sc in next 9 sc, sc2tog] across to top corner of left front, skip next sc, 3 sc in center sc of corner, sc in each sc down left front, turn.

Row 4: Ch 1, sc in each sc to top of left front, 3 sc in center sc of corner, skip next sc, [sc in next 8 sc, sc2tog] across to top corner of right front, skip next sc, 3 sc in center sc of corner, sc in each sc down right front, working 3 sc in each ch-3 space, turn.

Row 5: Ch 1, sc in each sc across to top of right front, 3 sc in corner st, skip next sc, sc in each sc across to 1 st before corner, skip next st, 3 sc in corner, sc in each sc down left front. Fasten off.

Finishing

Mark center of sleeve cap, pin sleeve in place centering on shoulder seam and easing into underarm. Sew sleeve in place.

Sew 4 buttons on left front opposite buttonholes. Sew one button at the top of each sleeve slit.

Lay garment on a padded surface, sprinkle with water, using rust proof pins, pin into shape, allow to dry. Do not press.

Skill Level

Intermediate

Yarn

Blue Sky Alpacas Sport Weight;
100% baby alpaca; 110 yds (100
m)/1.75 oz (50 g); #507 light gray:
8 (9, 11) skeins

kelley's island cardigan

It seems that ruffles are everywhere in clothing trends. In this case, a simple cardigan in a gorgeous yarn with an added ruffle takes a routine staple item in the closet and makes it something special. The ruffle is big enough to add flair, but small enough not to be fussy or pretentious. I can see myself wearing this sweater while eating lobster bisque after a relaxing vacation day lakeside.

Designed by
Ellen Gormley

Hooks	**Gauge**	**Notions**	**Finished Sizes**
8/H (5 mm)	2 pattern reps = 4½" (11.5 cm)	Yarn needle	Women's sizes S (M, L)
		Three 1" (2.5 cm) shank buttons	Finished bust: 36 (40, 45)" (91.5 [101.5, 114.5] cm)
		Two stitch markers	Finished length: 19½" (49.5 cm)

Reduced Sample of Pattern Stitch 1

Repeat

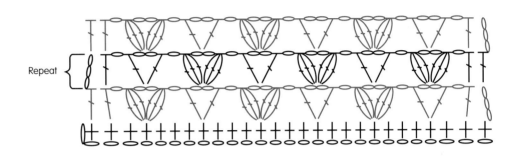

Reduced Sample of Pattern Stitch 2

Repeat

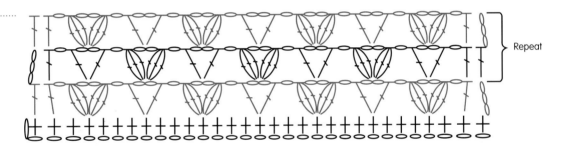

Special Stitches

Foundation single crochet (fsc): *Start with a slip knot, ch 2, insert hook in 2nd ch from hook, draw up a loop, yo, draw through 1 loop, yo, and draw through 2 loops – 1 single crochet with its own chain at bottom. Work next stitch under loops of that chain. Insert hook under 2 loops at bottom of the previous stitch, draw up a loop, yo and draw through 1 loop, yo and draw through 2 loops. Repeat for length of foundation.*

Cluster (Cl): *yarn over, insert hook in indicated stitch, yarn over and draw up a loop, yarn over and draw through 2 loops on hook (2 loops remain on hook), [yarn over, insert hook in same stitch, yarn over and draw up a loop, yarn over and draw through 2 loops on hook] twice, yarn over and draw through all 4 loops on hook.*

Cl shell: *(Cl, ch 2, Cl) in same st or space.*

V-St: *(Dc, ch 2, dc) in the same st or space.*

Pattern Stitch 1

Row 1 (RS): *Ch 3 (counts as dc here and throughout), skip first st, dc in next st, ch 1, skip next st, *Cl shell in next st, ch 1**, skip next 3 sts, V-st in next st, ch 1, skip next 3 sts; rep from * across, ending last rep at **, skip next st, dc in last 2 sts, turn.*

Row 2: *Ch 3, skip first st, dc in next st, *ch 1, skip next ch-1 space, V-st in next shell space, ch 1, skip next ch-1 space**, Cl-shell in next V-st sp; rep from * across, ending last rep at **, dc in last 2 dc, turn.*

Row 3: *Ch 3, skip first st, dc in next st, *ch 1, skip next ch-1 space, Cl-shell in next V-st space, ch 1, skip next ch-1 space**, V-st in next shell space; rep from * across, ending last rep at **, dc in last 2 dc, turn.*

Rep Rows 2-3 for pattern.

Pattern Stitch 2

Row 1 (RS): *Ch 3 (counts as dc here and throughout), skip first st, dc in next st, ch 1, skip next st, *V-st in next st, ch 1, skip next 3 sts, Cl-shell in next st, ch 1**, skip next 3 sts; rep from * across, ending last rep at **, ch 1, skip next st, dc in last 2 dc, turn.*

Row 2: *Ch 3, skip first st, dc in next st, *ch 1, skip next ch-1 space, V-st in next shell space, ch 1, skip next ch-1 space, Cl-shell in next V-st space; rep from * across to last ch-1 space, ch 1, skip next ch-1 space, dc in last 2 dc, turn.*

Rep Row 2 for pattern.

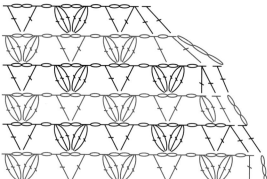
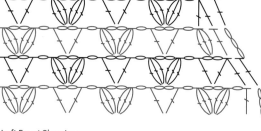

Left Front Shaping

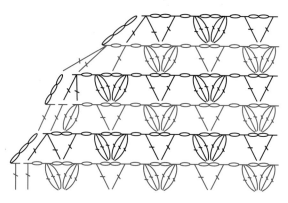

Right Front Shaping

Back

Work 63 (71, 79) Fsc.

Rows 1–29: Work even in pattern stitch 1. (7 [8, 9] pattern reps plus 1 Cl-shell on RS rows or 1 V-st on WS rows).

Left Front

Work 31 (35, 39) Fsc.

Sizes S and L Only

Rows 1–7: Work even in pattern stitch 1. (3 [4] pattern reps plus 1 Cl-shell on RS rows or 1 V-st on WS rows)

Sizes M Only

Rows 1–7: Work even in pattern stitch 2. (4 pattern reps)

All sizes

Row 8 (decrease): Ch 3, dc2tog over next dc and next ch-2 space, ch 2, dc in same ch-2 space, ch 1, skip next ch-1 space, work in pattern across, turn.

Row 9 (decrease): Work in pattern across, ending with Cl in ch-2 space of last V-st, dc in next dc2tog, dc in top of turning ch, turn.

Row 10 (decrease): Ch 3, dc2tog over next dc and next Cl, ch 1 skip next ch-1 space, work in pattern across, turn.

Row 11 (decrease): Work in pattern across, ending with dc in ch-2 space of last Cl-shell, ch 1, skip next ch-1 space, dc2tog over last 2 sts, turn.

Rows 12-15: Rep Rows 8-11 once.

Row 16: Ch 3, skip first st, dc in next dc, work in established pattern across, turn. (2 [2, 3] Cl-shells; 1 [1, 2] V-sts)

Rows 17-29: Work even in established pattern.

Fasten off leaving a 12" (30.5 cm) tail.

Right Front

Work same as left front through Row 7.

Row 8 (decrease): Work in established pattern across to last Cl-shell, dc in ch-2 space of last Cl-shell, ch 3, dc2tog working over same ch-2 space as last dc made and next dc, dc in last dc, turn.

Row 9: Ch 3, skip first st, dc in next dc-2tog, Cl in next ch-2 space, ch 1, skip next ch-1 space, work in pattern across, turn.

Row 10: Work in pattern across to last ch-1 space, ch 1, skip next ch-1 spac,e dc2tog over next Cl and next dc, dc in top of turning ch, turn.

Row 11: Ch 3, dc in next dc (counts a dc2tog), ch 1, skip next ch-1 space, dc in ch-2 space of next Cl-shell, work in pattern across, turn.

Rows 12-15: Rep Rows 8-11 once.

Row 16-29: Work even in pattern.

Fasten off leaving a 12" (30.5 cm) tail.

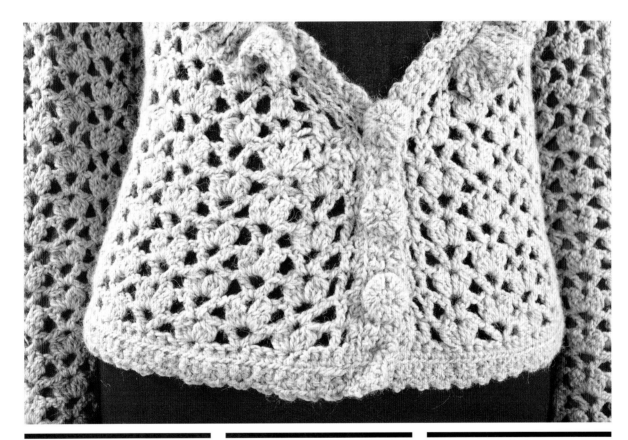

Sleeve

(Make 2)

Work 51 (55, 63) Fsc.

Size S Only

Rows 1–28: Work even in pattern stitch 2. (6 pattern reps) Fasten off leaving a long tail.

Sizes M and L Only

Rows 1–28: Work even in pattern stitch 1. (6 [7] pattern reps plus 1 Cl-shell on RS rows or 1 V-st on WS rows). Fasten off leaving a long tail.

Assembly

Block all pieces to correct measurements. Sew fronts to the back at shoulders.

Fold sleeve in half lengthwise, matching fold to shoulder seam, sew last row of sleeve to side of front and back. Sew side and underarm seam. Rep with other sleeve.

Sweater Edging

Row 1 (RS): With RS facing, join yarn with sc at bottom right-hand corner of right front, ch 1, working 2 sc in each row-end dc, sc evenly up front, across back neck edge and down left front edge, turn.

Row 2: Ch 1, working in front loop only, sc in each sc across, turn. (The unused back loop, visible on the RS will be used for the ruffle.)

Row 3 (buttonhole row): Ch 1, [sc in next 4 sts, ch 2, sk 2 sts] 3 times, sc in each remaining sc across, turn.

Row 4: Ch 1, *(sc, ch 2, sc) in next st, skip next st; rep from * across, ending with (sc, ch 2, sc) in last st. Fasten off.

Hem Edging

Row 1 (RS): With RS facing, working across opposite side of foundation ch, join yarn with sc in bottom left-hand corner of left front, sc evenly across, turn.

Row 2: Ch 1, working in front loops only, sc in each sc across, turn.

Note: The unused back loop, visible on the RS can be used for an optional ruffle (not shown).

Row 3: Ch 1, sc in each sc, turn.

Row 4: Ch 1, (sc, ch 2, sc) in first sc, *skip next st, (sc, ch 2, sc) in next st; rep from * across. Fasten off.

Sleeve Edging

Rnd 1: With RS facing, join yarn in seam on cuff edge of sleeve, ch 1, working across opposite side of foundation ch, sc in each ch around, join with Sl st in first sc.

Rnd 2: Ch 1, working in back loop only, sc in each sc around, join with Sl st in first sc.

Note: The unused front loop can be used for an optional ruffle (not shown).

Rnd 3: Ch 1, sc in both loops of each sc around, join with Sl st in first sc.

Rnd 4: Ch 1, (sc, ch 2, sc) in fist sc, skip next st, *(sc, ch 2, sc) in next sc, skip next st; rep from * around, join with Sl st in first sc. Fasten off.

Repeat on other sleeve.

Ruffle

Place a marker in 24th st from bottom
edge on right front and left front edges.
Working in unused loops of sts in Row
1 of hem edging, join yarn in marked st
on right front, ch 5 (counts as first dtr), 3
more dtr in same st, 4 dtr in each st up
right front, around neck and down left
front to next marked st. Fasten off.

Finishing

Weave in ends. Sew buttons on left front
opposite buttonholes.

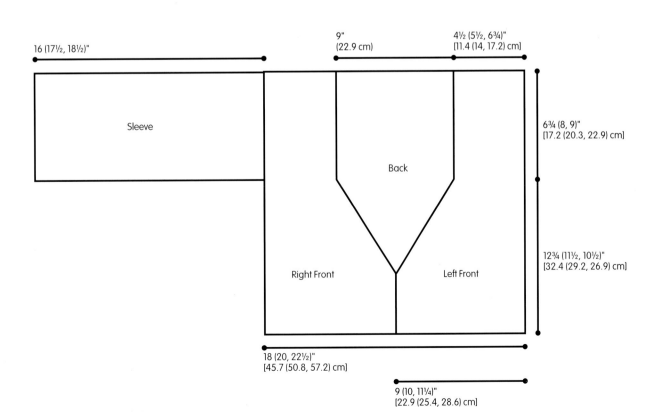

16 (17½, 18½)"

9"
(22.9 cm)

4½ (5½, 6¾)"
[11.4 (14, 17.2) cm]

Sleeve

Back

Right Front

Left Front

6¾ (8, 9)"
[17.2 (20.3, 22.9) cm]

12¾ (11½, 10½)"
[32.4 (29.2, 26.9) cm]

18 (20, 22½)"
[45.7 (50.8, 57.2) cm]

9 (10, 11¼)"
[22.9 (25.4, 28.6) cm]

Skill Level
Intermediate

Yarn
Plymouth Baby Alpaca Aire; 100%
baby alpaca; 218 yd (199 m)/3.5
oz (100 g); #5007 tans: 7 (8, 9, 9)
skeins

parisian swing coat

One of the amazing things about this little coat is how you feel when you put it on. The little swing of the body and the loose fitting sleeves seem to put a swing in your step, as if you were a model walking down a runway. Also amazing is that the yarn—a bulky, 100% baby alpaca—worked with a large hook is surprisingly very light in weight.

Designed by
Margaret Hubert

Hooks
10½/K (6.5 mm)

9/I (5.5 mm)

Gauge
11 sts and 9 rows hdc = 4" (10 cm) with 10½/K (6.5 mm) hook

12 sc = 4" (10 cm) with 9/I (5.5 mm) hook

Notions
Yarn needle

Three 2" (5 cm) buttons

Four stitch markers

Finished Sizes
Women's sizes S (M, L, XL)

Finished bust: 43 (44½, 45½, 47)" (109 [113, 115.5, 119.5] cm)

Finished length: 26½" (67.5 cm)

Reduced Sample of Pattern

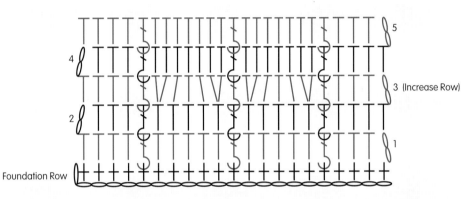

Special Stitches

Front post double crochet (FPdc): *Yo, insert hook from front to back to front again around the post of next st, yo, draw yarn through st, [yo, draw yarn through 2 loops on hook] twice.*

Back post double crochet (BPdc): *Yo, insert hook from back to front to back again around the post of next st, yo, draw yarn through st, [yo, draw yarn through 2 loops on hook] twice.*

Sc2tog: *[Insert hook in next st, yo, draw yarn through st] twice, yo, draw yarn through 3 loops on hook*

Yoke

Starting at neck edge with 10½/K hook, ch 90 (94, 98, 102),

Foundation Row: Sc in 2nd ch from hook and in each ch across, turn. (89 [93, 97, 101] sc)

Row 1 (RS): Ch 2 (counts as hdc here and throughout), skip first sc, hdc in each of the next 1 (3, 5, 7) sc, FPdc around the post of next sc, [hdc in next 5 sc, FPdc around the post of next sc] 14 times, hdc in each of last 2 (4, 6, 8) sc, turn. (15 raised ribs)

Row 2 (WS): Ch 2, hdc in each of the next 1 (3, 5, 7) hdc, BPdc around the post of next FPdc, [hdc in each of the next 5 hdc, BPdc around the post of next FPdc] 14 times, hdc in each of last 2 (4, 6, 8) hdc, turn.

Row 3 (increase row): Ch 2, hdc in each of the next 1 (3, 5, 7) hdc, FPdc around the post of next BPdc, [2 hdc in next hdc (inc made), hdc in each hdc across to last hdc of group, 2 hdc in last hdc (inc made), FPdc around the post of next BPdc] 14 times, hdc in each of the last 2 (4, 6, 8) hdc, turn. (117 [121, 125, 129] sts)

Row 4: Ch 2, hdc in each of the next 1 (3, 5, 7) hdc, BPdc around the post of next FPdc, [hdc in each hdc across to next post st, BPdc around the post of next FPdc] 14 times, hdc in each of the last 2 (4, 6, 8) hdc, turn.

Row 5: Ch 2, hdc in each of next 1 (3, 5, 7) hdc, FPdc around the post of next BPdc, [hdc in each hdc across to next post st, FPdc around the post of next BPdc] 14 times, hdc in each of the last 2 (4, 6, 8) hdc, turn.

Rows 6–8: Repeat Rows 4–5 once; then rep Row 4 once.

Rows 9–20: Repeat Rows 3–8 twice, following established pattern and increasing on Row 3 before and after raised ribs as before. (173 [177, 181, 185] sts at end of last row)

Row 21 (increase row): Ch 2, hdc in each of next 1 (3, 5, 7) hdc, FPdc around the post of next BPdc, *[(2 hdc in next hdc, hdc in next 4 hdc) twice, 2 hdc in next hdc, FPdc around the post of next BPdc] twice*, [2 hdc in next hdc, hdc in each hdc to last hdc of group, 2 hdc in last hdc, FPdc around the post of next BPdc] 10 times; rep from * once, hdc in last 2 (4, 6, 8) hdc, turn. (205 [209, 213, 217] sts)

Mark for Armholes as Follows:

With RS facing, place a marker in the 26th (28th, 30th, 31st) st (marks the right front), place a marker in 40th st from last marker (marks the sleeve), place a marker in 73rd st from last marker (marks the back), count 39 sts from marker, place a marker in 40th st from last marker (marks the sleeve), there should be 26 (28, 30, 32) sts remaining at end of row for left front.

Row 22: Work even in pattern to first marked st, 2 hdc in marked st, skip next 39 sts for sleeve, 2 hdc in the next marked st, continue in pattern across next 72 sts of back, 2 hdc in next marked st, skip next 39 sts for sleeve, 2 hdc in the next marked st, continue in pattern across last 26 (28, 30, 32) sts, turn. (129 [133, 137, 141] sts for body)

Rows 23–30: Work even in pattern as established.

Row 31 (increase row): Ch 2, hdc in each of next 1 (3, 5, 7) hdc, FPdc around the post of next BPdc, [2 hdc in next hdc, hdc in each hdc to the next post st, FPdc around the post of next BPdc] 8 times, hdc in last 2 (4, 6, 8) hdc, turn. (139, 141, 143, 145 sts)

Rows 32-40: Work even in established pattern.

Row 41 (increase row): Ch 2, hdc in next 1 (3, 5, 7) hdc, FPdc around the post of next BPdc, (2 hdc in next hdc, hdc to last hdc of group, 2 hdc in last hdc, FPdc around the post of next BPdc) 8 times, hdc in last 3 hdc, turn. (153 [157, 161, 165)

Rows 42-52: Work even in established pattern. Fasten off.

Sleeve

(Make 2)

With WS facing, join new yarn with sl st in unworked st next to marker

Row 1 (WS): With WS facing, join yarn in first unworked st to the left of marker in armhole opening, ch 2, hdc in same st, [hdc in each hdc across to next post st, BPdc around the post of next FPdc] 3 times, hdc in each hdc across to last st before next marker, 2 hdc in last hdc, turn. (38 hdc, 3 raised ribs)

Rows 2-9: Work even in pattern as established.

Row 10 (increase row): Ch 2, [hdc in each hdc to last hdc of group, 2 hdc in last hdc, FPdc around the post of next BPdc] 3 times, 2 hdc in next hdc, hdc in each hdc around, turn. (42 hdc, 3 raised ribs)

Rows 11-19: Work even in established pattern, turn.

Row 20 (increase row): Repeat Row 10, turn. (46 hdc, 3 raised ribs).

Rows 21–31: Work even in established pattern. Fasten off.

Collar

Row 1: With RS facing, with 9/I hook, join yarn in first ch on opposite side of foundation ch, ch 1, sc in each ch across, turn. (89 [93, 97, 101] sc)

Row 2: Ch 1, sc in first sc, sc2tog, sc in each of the next 3 (7, 8, 8) sc, sc2tog, [sc in each of the next 8 sc, sc2tog] 8 times, sc in each of last 1 (1, 4, 8) sc, turn. (79 [83, 87, 91] sc)

Row 3: Ch 1, sc in each sc across, turn.

Row 4: Ch 1, sc in the first sc, sc2tog, sc in each of the next 1 (5, 7, 7) sc, sc2tog, [sc in each of the next 7 sc, sc2tog] 8 times, sc in each of the last 1 (1, 3, 7) sc, turn. (69 [73, 77, 81] sc)

Row 5: Ch 1, sc in each sc across row, turn.

Row 6: Ch 1, sc in first sc, sc2tog, sc in each of the next 5 (3, 5, 6) sc, sc2tog, [sc in each of the next 6 sc, sc2tog] 8 times, sc in each of the last 3 (1, 3, 6) sc, turn. (59 [63, 67, 71] sc)

Rows 7-10: Rep Row 5.

Row 11: Ch 1, working in back loops only, sc in each sc across, turn.

Rows 12-17: Rep Row 5.

Row 18 (increase row): Ch 1, sc in each of the next 2 (4, 6, 8) sc, sc in next sc, [sc in each of the next 5 sc, 2 sc in next sc] 9 times, sc in each of the last 2 (4, 6, 8) sc, turn. (69 [73, 77, 81] sc)

Row 19: Rep Row 5.

Row 20 (increase row): Ch 1, sc in each of the next 2 (4, 6, 8) sc [sc in each of the next 6 sc, 2 sc in next sc] 9 times, sc in each of the last 3 (5, 7, 9) sc, turn. (79 [83, 87, 91] sc)

Row 21: Ch 1, sc in each sc across row. Fasten off, leaving a long sewing length. Fold collar in half towards the inside of jacket at Row 11, sew down along neckline.

Button Bands

Before starting button bands, divide fronts into 4 quarters, marking each section.

Left Front Button Band

Row 1: With RS facing, with 9/I hook, working through both thicknesses of collar, join yarn in top left-hand corner of left front edge, ch 1, work 15 sc evenly spaced across each quarter of left front to bottom left-hand corner, turn. (60 sc)

Rows 2-4: Ch 1, sc in each sc across, turn. Fasten off.

Right Front Buttonhole Band

Row 1: With RS facing, with 9/I hook, join yarn in bottom right-hand corner of right front edge, ch 1, work 15 sc evenly spaced across each quarter of right front to top right-hand corner, turn. (60 sc)

Row 2: Ch 1, sc in each sc across, turn.

Row 3 (buttonhole row): Ch 1, sc in each of the next 34 sc, [ch 4, skip 3 sc, sc in each of the next 6 sc] twice, ch 4, skip next 3 sc, sc in each of the last 5 sc, turn. (3 buttonholes made)

Row 4: Ch 1, sc in each sc across, working 3 sc in each ch-4 buttonhole loop, turn.

Row 5: Ch 1, sc in each sc across to top right-hand corner, 3 sc in last sc to turn corner, sc in each st along top of collar, 3 sc in last st to turn corner, sc in each sc across left front edge, do not turn.

Row 6: Working from left to right, ch 1, reverse sc in each sc across left front, collar, and right front. Fasten off.

Finishing

Sew underarm seams.

Raised Rib

With RS facing, join yarn around the post of first post st in Row 1 of first raised rib, working around posts of post sts, sc loosely across to bottom edge to accentuate the ribbed look. Fasten off.

Rep raised rib row across each raised rib.

Weave in ends. Sew buttons to left front opposite buttonholes.

Lay garment on a padded surface, using rust proof pins, pin into shape, sprinkle lightly with water, allow to dry.

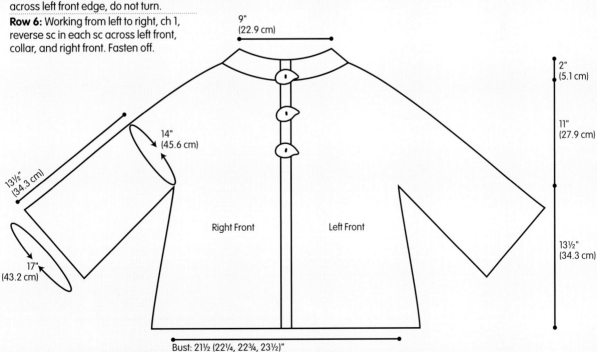

9"
(22.9 cm)

2"
(5.1 cm)

11"
(27.9 cm)

14"
(45.6 cm)

13½"
(34.3 cm)

17"
(43.2 cm)

Right Front

Left Front

13½"
(34.3 cm)

Bust: 21½ (22¼, 22¾, 23½)"
[54.6 (56.5, 57.8, 59.7) cm]

Bottom: 25½ (26, 27, 27½)"
[64.8 (66, 68.6, 69.9) cm]

ripples asymmetrical top

Diagonals are dramatic and figure-flattering. This top, with a cascade of ripples down the right hip, can easily go from daytime casual to evening chic.

Skill Level
Intermediate

Yarn
Patons Silk Bamboo; 70% viscose from bamboo, 30% silk; 102 yd (93 m)/2.2 oz (65 g), #85607 saffron: 9 (10,11) balls

Designed by
Tatyana Mirer

Hooks	Gauge	Notions	Finished Sizes
6/G (4 mm)	5 ripples = 10½" (26.5 cm); 8 rows in body pattern = 4" (10 cm); 6 rows in bodice pattern = 2½".	Yarn needle Markers	Women's sizes S (M, L) Finished bust: 34 (38, 42)" (86.5 [96.5, 106.5] cm) Finished length: 28½ (29½, 33½)" (72.5 [75, 85] cm)

Reduced sample of back pattern

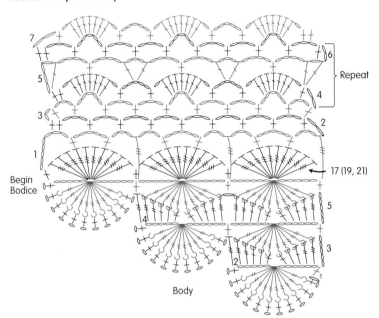

Back

Body

Row 1: Work 11 Fsc, turn.

Row 2 (WS): Ch 5, FPtr10tog in next 10 sts, ch 6, sc in top of turning ch, turn. (1 cluster).

Row 3 (extended row): Ch 5 (counts as dtr), skip first st, dtr in next ch, tr in next ch, dc in next ch, hdc in next ch, sc in next ch, skip next ch and next cluster, sc in next ch, hdc in next ch, dc in next ch, tr in next ch, dtr in last st, dtr in last st, work extended Fsc as follows: ch 1, insert hook in top of dtr just made, yo, draw through 1 loop, yo, and draw through 2 loops (first Fsc made), work 10 Fsc, turn. (1 ripple; 11 Fsc)

Row 4: Skip first st, *ch 5, FPtr10tog in next 10 sts, ch 6, sc in next dtr; rep from * across, turn. (2 clusters)

Row 5 (extended row): Ch 5, skip first st, *dtr in next ch, tr in next ch, dc in next ch, hdc in next ch, sc in next ch, skip next ch and next cluster, sc in next ch, hdc in next ch, dc in next ch, tr in next ch, dtr in next ch**, ch 1, skip next sc; rep from * across, ending last rep at **, dtr in last st, work first extended Fsc as before, work 10 Fsc, turn. (2 ripples; 11 Fsc)

Row 6: Skip first st, *ch 5, FPtr10tog in next 10 sts, ch 6, sc in next dtr; rep from * across, turn. (3 clusters)

Rows 7–16 (18, 20): Repeat Rows 5–6 (5 [6, 7] times. (8 [9, 10] clusters at end of last row)

Row 17 (19, 21): *Skip next ch-5 space, 10 dtr in center ch of previous row, skip next ch-5 space, sc in next sc; rep from * across, turn. Do not fasten off.

Special Stitches

Foundation single crochet (fsc): Start with a slip knot, ch 2, insert hook in 2nd ch from hook, draw up a loop, yo, draw through 1 loop, yo, and draw through 2 loops—1 single crochet with its own ch at bottom. Work next stitch under loops of that ch. Insert hook under 2 loops at bottom of the previous stitch, draw up a loop, yo and draw through 1 loop, yo and draw through 2 loops. Repeat for length of foundation.

FPdc10tog: *Yo (twice), insert hook from front to back to front again around the post of next st, yo, draw yarn through, [yo draw yarn through 2 loops on hook] twice; rep from * 9 times; yo, draw yarn through 11 loops on hook.

V-stitch (V-st): (Dc, ch 3, dc) in same st or space.

Dc2tog: [Yo, insert hook in next st or sp, yo, draw yarn through st, yo, draw yarn through 2 loops on hook] twice, yo, draw yarn through 3 loops on hook.

Sc3tog: [Insert hook in next st, yo, draw yarn through st] 3 times, yo, draw yarn through 4 loops on hook.

How to make a gauge swatch

Ch 23 (loosely).

Row 1: Sc in 2nd ch and in each ch across, turn. (22 sc)

Row 2: [Ch 5, FPtr10tog in next 10 sc, ch 6, sc in next sc] twice, turn. (2 clusters)

Row 3: Ch 5 (counts as dtr), skip first st, *dtr in next ch, tr in next ch, dc in next ch, hdc in next ch, sc in next ch, skip next ch and next cluster, sc in next ch, hdc in next ch, dc in next ch, tr in next ch, dtr in next ch*, ch 1, skip next sc; rep from * to * once, dtr in last st, turn. (2 ripples)

Row 4: Ch 5 (count as dtr), skip first dtr, *FPtr10tog in next 10 sts, ch 6*, sc in next ch-1 space, ch 5; rep from * to * once, sc in top of turning ch, turn. (2 clusters)

Rows 5–8: Rep Rows 3–4 twice.

Gauge swatch should measure 4 ¼ x 4" (11 x 10 cm).

Reduced Sample of Front Pattern

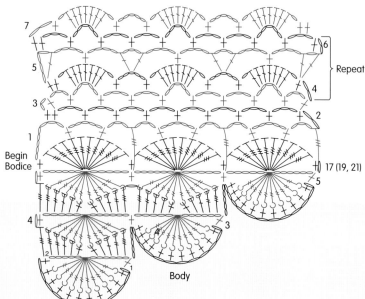

Bodice

Row 1 (WS): Ch 5 (counts as dtr), *ch 3, skip next 3 dtr, sc in next dtr, ch 5, skip next 2 dtr, sc in next dtr, ch 3, skip next 3 dtr, long dtr in sc 2 rows below; rep from * across, turn. (8 [9, 10] ch-5 spaces; 16 [18, 20] ch-3 spaces)

Row 2: Ch 2, *sc in next ch-3 space, ch 3, sc in next ch-5 space, ch 3**, sc in next ch-3 space, ch 3; rep from * across, ending last rep at **, 2 sc in last ch-3 space, turn. (23 [26, 29] ch-3 spaces)

Row 3: Ch 2, skip first sc, sc in next sc, *ch 3, sc in next ch-3 space, ch 5, sc in next ch-3 space, ch 3**, sc in next ch-3 space; rep from * across, ending last rep at **, sc in last sc, turn.

Row 4: Ch 2, *sc in next ch-3 space, ch 1, 7 dc in next ch-5 space, ch 1, sc in next ch-3 space**, ch 5; rep from * across, ending last rep at **, 2 sc in last ch-3 space, turn.

Row 5: Ch 4 (counts as dc, ch 1), dc in first st, *ch 4, skip next 3 dc, sc in next dc, ch 4**, V-st in next ch-5 space; rep from * across, ending last rep at **, (dc, ch 1, dc) in last sc, turn.

Row 6: Ch 2, sc in next ch-1 space, *ch 3, sc in next ch-4 space, ch 5, sc in next ch-4 space, ch 3**, sc in next ch-3 space; rep from * across, ending last rep at **, sc in last ch-1 space, sc in 3rd ch of turning ch, turn.

Rows 7-17 (19, 20): Rep Rows 4–6 (3 [3, 4] times); then rep Rows 4–5 once.

Shape Armhole

Row 1: Sl st in each of first 13 sts, ch 1, sc in next ch-3 space, *ch 3, sc in next ch-4 space, ch 5, sc in next ch-4 space, ch 3, sc in next ch-3 space; rep from * across to last 13 sts, turn, leaving rem sts unworked.

Rows 2–24 (24, 27): Work bodice rows 4–6 (7 [7, 8] times); then rep Rows 4–5 once. Fasten off.

Front

Body

Ch 12 (loosely).

Row 1: Sc in 2nd ch and in each ch across, turn. (11 sc)

Row 2 (WS): Ch 5, skip first st, FPtr10tog in next 10 sts, ch 6, sc in top of turning ch, turn. (1 cluster)

Row 3 (extended row): Ch 16 (loosely) (counts as dtr, ch 12 for next ripple), sc in 2nd ch from hook and in each of next 9 ch sts (forms first ripple), skip 5 ch (for dtr) and next sc, dtr in next ch, tr in next ch, dc in next ch, hdc in next ch, sc in next ch, skip next ch and next cluster, sc in next ch, hdc in next ch, dc in next ch, tr in next ch, dtr in next ch, dtr in last st, turn. (2 ripples)

Row 4: Ch 1, sc in first dtr, ch 5, FPtr10tog in next 10 sts, ch 6, sc in 5th ch of ch-16 of previous row, ch 5, FPtr10tog in next 10 sts, ch 6, sc in top of turning ch, turn.

Row 5 (extended row): Ch 16 (loosely) (counts as dtr, ch 12 for next ripple), sc in 2nd ch from hook and in each of next 9 ch sts (forms first ripple), skip 5 ch (for dtr) and next sc, *dtr in next ch, tr in next ch, dc in next ch, hdc in next ch, sc in next ch, skip next ch and next cluster, sc in next ch, hdc in next ch, dc in next ch, tr in next ch, dtr in next ch**, ch 1, skip next sc; rep from * across, ending last rep at **, dtr in last st, turn. (3 ripples)

Row 6: Ch 1, sc in first dtr, *ch 5, FPtr10tog in next 10 sts, ch 6, sc in next dtr; rep from * across, working next to the last sc in 5th ch of ch-16 of previous row, and ending with slast sc in top of turning ch, turn. (3 clusters)

Rows 7-16 (18, 20): Repeat Rows 5–6 (5 [6, 7] times). (8 [9, 10] clusters at end of last row)

Row 17 (19, 21): *Skip next ch-5 space, 10 dtr in center ch of previous row, skip next ch-5 space, sc in next sc; rep from * across, turn. Do not fasten off.

Bodice

Work same as back bodice through Row 1 of armhole shaping.

Rows 2–5: Work back bodice Rows 4–6 once; then rep Row 4 once.

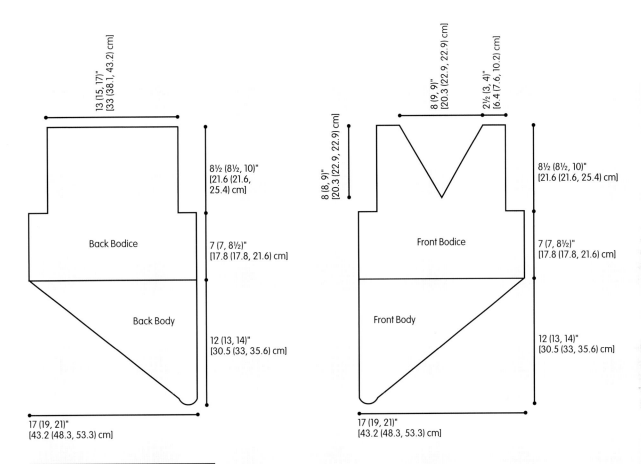

Left Front Neck and Armhole Shaping

Sizes S and L Only

Row 1 (RS): Ch 4 (counts as dc, ch 1 here and throughout out), dc in first st, [ch 4, skip next 3 dc, sc in next dc, ch 4, V-st in next ch-5 space] 2 (3) times, ch 4, skip next 3 dc, sc in next dc, ch 4, dc in next ch-5 space, turn, leaving remaining sts unworked. (2 [3] V-sts)

Row 2: Ch 2, [sc in next ch-4 space, ch 5, sc in next ch-4 space, ch 3, sc in next ch-3 space, ch 3] 2 (3) times, sc in last st, turn. (2 [3] ch-5 spaces)

Row 3: Ch 2, [sc in next ch-3 space, ch 1, 7 dc in next ch-5 space, ch 1, sc in next ch-3 space, ch 5] 2 (3) times, sc in next ch-3 space, ch 1, 3 dc in next ch-5 space, dc2tog, working in same ch-5 space and in last sc, turn.

Row 4: Ch 2, skip first 2 sts, sc in next st, [ch 4, V-st in next ch-5 space, ch 4, skip next 3 dc, sc in next dc] 2 (3) times, ch 4, (dc, ch 1, dc) in last sc, turn.

Row 5: Ch 2, sc in first ch-1 space, [ch 3, sc in next ch-4 space, ch 5, sc in next ch-4 space, ch 3, sc in next ch-3 space] 2 (3) times, ch 3, sc in last ch-4 space, dc in top of turning ch, turn.

Row 6: Ch 3, [sc in next ch-3 space, ch 5, sc in next ch-3 space, ch 1, 7 dc in next ch-5 space, ch 1] 2 (3) times, sc in last ch-3 space, sc in last sc, turn.

Row 7: Ch 4, dc in first st, [ch 4, skip next 3 dc, sc in next dc, ch 4, V-st in next ch-5 space] 1 (2) times, ch 4, skip next 3 dc, sc in next dc, ch 4, dc in next ch-5 space, ch 3, dc2tog, working in same ch-5 space and in top of turning ch, turn.

Row 8: Ch 2, [sc in next ch-3 space, ch 3, sc in next ch-4 space, ch 5, sc in next ch-4 space, ch 3, sc in next ch-3 space] 1 (2) times, ch 3, sc in next ch-4 space, ch 5, sc in next ch-4 space, ch 3, sc in next ch-1 space, sc in last sc, turn.

Row 9: Ch 2, [sc in next ch-3 space, ch 1, 7 dc in next ch-5 space, ch 1, sc in next ch-3 space, ch 5] 1 (2) times, ch 1, 7 dc in next ch-5 space, ch 1, dc in top of turning ch, turn.

Row 10: Ch 3, dc in first st, [ch 4, skip next 3 dc, sc in next dc, ch 4, V-st in next ch-5 space] 1 (2) times, ch 4, skip next 3 dc, sc in next dc, ch 4, (dc, ch 1, dc) in last sc, turn.

Row 11: Ch 2, sc in next ch-1 space, [ch 3, sc in next ch-4 space, ch 5, sc in next ch-4 space, ch 3, sc in next ch-3 space] 1 (2) times, ch 3, sc in next ch-4 space, ch 5, sc in next ch-4 space, sc in top of turning ch, turn.

Row 12: Ch 3, 4 dc in next ch-5 space, [ch 1, sc in next ch-3 space, ch 5, sc in next ch-3 space, ch 1, 7 dc in next ch-5 space] 1 (2) times, ch 1, sc in next ch-3 space, sc in last sc, turn.

Row 13: Ch 4, dc in first st, [ch 4, skip next 3 dc, sc in next dc, ch 4, V-st in next ch-5 space] 1 (2) times, ch 4, skip next 2 dc, sc in next dc, ch 1, dc in top of turning ch, turn.

Row 14: Ch 2, sc in first st, [ch 5, sc in c next h-4 space, ch 3, sc in next ch-3 space, ch 3, sc in next ch-4 space] 1 (2) times, ch 5, sc in next ch-4 space, ch 3, sc in next ch-1 space, sc in last sc, turn.

Row 15: Ch 2, [sc in next ch-3 space, ch 1, 7 dc in next ch-5 space, ch 1, sc in next ch-3 space, ch 5] 1 (2) times, sc in next ch-3 space, ch 1, 2 dc in next ch-5 space, turn.

Row 16: Ch 5, [V-st in next ch-5 space, ch 4, skip next 3 dc, sc in next dc, ch 4] 1 (2) times, (dc, ch 1, dc) in last sc, turn.

Size S Only

Row 17: Ch 2, sc in next ch-1 space, ch 3, sc in next ch-4 space, ch 5, sc in next ch-4 space, ch 3, sc in next ch-3 space, ch 1, dc in top of turning ch, turn.

Row 18: Ch 2, sc in next ch-3 space, ch 1, 7 dc in ch-5 space, ch 1, sc in next ch-3 space, sc in last sc, sc in top of turning ch, turn.

Row 19: Ch 4, dc in first st, ch 4, skip next 3 dc, sc in next dc, ch 4, (dc, ch 1, dc) in last sc. Fasten off.

Size L Only

Row 17: Ch 2, sc in next ch-1 space, ch 3, sc in next ch-4 space, ch 5, sc in next ch-4 space, ch 3, sc in next ch-3 space, ch 3, sc in next ch-4 space, ch 5, sc in next ch-4 space, ch 3, sc in next ch-3 space, ch 1, dc in top of turning ch, turn.

Row 18: Ch 2, sc in next ch-3 space, ch 1, 7 dc in next ch-5 space, ch 1, sc in next ch-3 space, ch 5, sc in next ch-3 space, ch 1, 7 dc in next ch-5 space, ch 1, sc in next ch-3 space, sc in last sc, turn.

Row 19: Ch 4, dc in first st, ch 4, skip next 3 dc, sc in next dc, ch 4, V-st in next ch-5 space, ch 4, skip 3 next dc, sc in next dc, ch 4, (dc, ch 1, dc) in top of turning ch, turn.

Row 20–22: Rep Rows 17-19 once. Fasten off.

Size M Only

Row 1 (RS): Ch 4, dc in first st, [ch 4, skip next 3 dc, sc in next dc, ch 4, V-st in next ch-5 space] 3 times, skip next 3 dc, tr in next dc, turn.

Row 2: Ch 5, [sc in next ch-3 space, ch 3, sc in next ch-4 space, ch 5, sc in next ch-4 space, ch 3] 3 times, sc in last ch-1 space, sc in 3rd ch of turning ch, turn.

Row 3: Ch 2, [sc in next ch-3 space, ch 1, 7 dc in next ch-5 space, ch 1, sc in next ch-3 space, ch 5] twice, sc in next ch-3 space, ch 1, 7 dc in next ch-5 space, ch 1, sc in next ch-3 space, ch 2, dc in 3rd ch of turning ch, turn,

Row 4: Ch 5, [skip next 3 dc, sc in next st, ch 4, V-st in next ch-5 space, ch 4] twice, skip next 3 dc, sc in next dc, ch 4, (dc, ch 1, dc) in last sc, turn.

Row 5: Ch 2, sc in next ch-1 space, [ch 3, sc in next ch-4 space, ch 5, sc in next ch-4 space, ch 3, sc in next ch-3 space] twice, ch 3, sc in next ch-4 space, ch 5, sc in turning ch-5 space, ch 1, dc in 3rd ch of turning ch, turn.

Row 6: Ch 1, sc in next ch-1 space, [ch 1, 7 dc in next ch-5 space, ch 1, sc in next ch-3 space, ch 5, sc in next ch-3 space] twice, ch 1, 7 dc in next ch-5 space, ch 1, sc in last ch-3 space, sc in last sc, turn.

Row 7: Ch 4, dc in first st, [ch 4, skip next 3 dc, sc in next dc, ch 4, V-st in next ch-5 space] twice, ch 4, skip next 3 dc, sc in each of next 2 dc, turn.

Row 8: Ch 5, [sc in next ch-4 space, ch 3, sc in next ch-3 space, ch 3, sc in next ch-4 space, ch 5] twice, sc in next ch-4 space, ch 3, sc in next ch-1 space, sc in 3rd ch of ch-4 turning ch, turn.

Row 9: Ch 2, [sc in next ch-3 space, ch 1, 7 dc in next ch-5 space, ch 1, sc in next ch-3 space, ch 5] twice, sc in next ch-3 space, ch 1, 3 dc in next ch-5 space, turn.

Row 10: Ch 5, [V-st in next ch-5 space, ch 4, skip next 3 dc, sc in next dc, ch 4] twice, (dc, ch 1, dc) in last sc, turn.

Row 11: Ch 2, sc in next ch-1 space, [ch 3, sc in next ch-4 space, ch 5, sc in next ch-4 space, ch 3, sc in next ch-3 space] twice, sc in top of ch-5 turning ch, turn.

Row 12: Ch 5, sc in next ch-3 space, ch 1, 7 dc in next ch-5 space, ch 1, sc in next ch-3 space, ch 5, sc in next ch-3 space, ch 1, 7 dc in next ch-5 space, ch 1, sc in next ch-3 space, sc in last sc, turn.

Row 13: Ch 4, dc in first st, ch 4, skip next 3 dc, sc in next dc, ch 4, V-st in next ch-5 space, ch 4, skip next 3 dc, sc in next dc, ch 4, dc in top of ch-5 turning ch, turn.

Row 14: Ch 2, sc in next ch-4 space, ch 5, sc in next ch-4 space, ch 3, sc in next ch-3 space, ch 3, sc in next ch-4 space, ch 5, sc in next ch-4 space, ch 3, sc in next ch-1 space, sc in 3rd ch of ch-4 turning ch, turn.

Row 15: Ch 2, sc in next ch-3 space, ch 1, 7 dc in next ch-5 space, ch 1, sc in next ch-3 space, ch 5, sc in next ch-3 space, ch 1, 7 dc in next ch-5 space, ch 1, sc in top of turning ch, turn.

Row 16: Ch 7, skip next 3 dc, sc in next dc, ch 4, V-st in next ch-5 space, ch 4, skip next 3 dc, sc in next dc, ch 4, (dc, ch 1, dc) in last sc, turn.

Row 17: Ch 2, sc in next ch-1 space, ch 3, sc in next ch-4 space, ch 5, sc in next ch-4 space, ch 3, sc in next ch-3 space, ch 3, sc in next ch-4 space, ch 5, sc in top of turning ch, turn.

Row 18: Ch 3, 5 dc in next ch-5 space, ch 1, sc in next ch-3 space, ch 5, sc in next ch-3 space, ch 1, 7 dc in next ch-5 space, ch 1, sc in next ch-3 space, sc in last sc, turn.

Row 19: Ch 4, dc in first st, ch 4, skip next 3 dc, sc in next dc, ch 4, V-st in next ch-5 space, ch 4, skip next 4 dc, sc in each of next dc, sc in top of turning ch, turn. Fasten off.

Right Front Neck and Armhole Shaping

Sizes S and L Only

Row 1: With RS facing, join yarn in center ch-5 space (already holding last st of Row 1 of left front), ch 7, [skip next 3 dc, sc in next dc, ch 4, V-st in next ch-5 space, ch 4] 2 (3) times, skip next 3 dc, sc in next dc, ch 4, (dc, ch 1, dc) in last st, turn.

Row 2: Ch 2, sc in next ch-1 space, [ch 3, sc in next ch-4 space, ch 5, sc in next ch-4 space, ch 3, sc in next ch-3 space] 2 (3) times, ch 3, sc in next ch-4 space, ch 5, sc in 3rd ch of turning ch, turn.

Row 3: Ch 3, 3 dc in next ch-5 space, [ch 1, sc in next ch-3 space, ch 5, sc in next ch-3 space, ch 1, 7 dc in next ch-5 space] 2(3) times, ch 1, sc in next ch-3 space, turn.

Row 4: Ch 4, dc in first st, [ch 4, skip next 3 dc, sc in next dc, ch 4, V-st in next ch-5 space] 2 (3) times, ch 4, sc in top of ch-3 turning ch, turn.

Row 5: Ch 4, sc in next ch-4 space, [ch 3, sc in next ch-3 space, ch 3, sc in next ch-4 space, ch 5, sc in next ch-4 space] 2 (3) times, ch 3, sc in 3rd ch of turning ch, turn.

Row 6: Ch 2, [sc in next ch-3 space, ch 1, 7 dc in next ch-5 space, ch 1, sc in next ch-3 space, ch 5] 2 (3) times, sc in last ch-3 space, dc in top of turning ch, turn.

Row 7: Ch 3, [V-st in next ch-5 space, ch 4, skip next 3 dc, sc in next dc, ch 4] 1 (2) times, V-st in next ch-5 space, ch 4, skip next 3 dc, sc in next dc, ch 4, (dc, ch 1, dc) in last sc, turn.

Row 8: Ch 2, sc in next ch-1 space, [ch 3, sc in next ch-4 space, ch 5, sc in next ch-4 space, ch 3, sc in next ch-3 space] 1 (2) times, ch 3, sc in next ch-4 space, ch 5, sc in next ch-4 space, ch 3, sc in next ch-3 space, turn.

Row 9: Ch 2, [sc in next ch-3 space, ch 1, 7 dc in next ch-5 space, ch 1, sc in next ch-3 space, ch 5] 1 (2) times, sc in next ch-3 space, ch 1, 7 dc in next ch-5 space, ch 1, sc in next ch-3 space, sc in last st, turn.

Row 10: Ch 4, dc in first st, [ch 4, skip next 3 dc, sc in next dc, ch 4, V-st in next ch-5 space] 1 (2) times, ch 4, skip next 3 dc, sc in next dc, ch 2, dc in turning ch, turn.

Row 11: Ch 2, sc in next ch-2 space, [ch 5, sc in next ch-4 space, ch 3, sc in next ch-3 space, ch 3, sc in next ch-4 space] 1 (2) times, ch 5, sc in next ch-4 space, ch 3, sc in next ch-1 space, sc in 3rd ch of turning ch, turn.

Row 12: Ch 2, [sc in next ch-3 space, ch 1, 7 dc in next ch-5 space, ch 1, sc in next ch-3 space, ch 5] 1 (2) times, sc in next ch-3 space, ch 1, 3 dc in next ch-5 space, dc2tog working in same ch-5 space and in top of turning ch, turn.

Row 13: Ch 1, sc in first st, [ch 4, V-st in next ch-5 space, ch 4, skip next 3 dc, sc in next dc] 1 (2) times, ch 4, (dc, ch 1, dc) in last sc, turn.

Row 14: Ch 2, sc in next ch-1 space, [ch 3, sc in next ch-4 space, ch 5, sc in next ch-4 space, ch 3, sc in next ch-3 space] 1 (2) times, ch 3, sc in next ch-4 space, sc in last sc, turn.

Row 15: Ch 3, dc in first st, [ch 1, sc in next ch-3 space, ch 5, sc in next ch-3 space, ch 1, 7 dc in next ch-5 space, ch 1] 1 (2) times, sc in next ch-3 space, sc in last sc, turn.

Row 16: Ch 4, dc in first st, [ch 4, skip next 3 dc, sc in next dc, ch 4, V-st in next ch-5 space] 1 (2) times, ch 1, dc in top of ch-3 turning ch, turn.

Size S Only

Row 17: Ch 2, sc in ch-1 space, ch 3, sc in next ch-3 space, ch 3, sc in next ch-4 space, ch 5, sc in next ch-4 space, ch 3, sc in ch-1 space. Turn.

Row 18: Ch 2, sc in ch-3 space, ch 1, 7 dc in ch-5 space, ch 1, sc in next ch-3 space, sc in last ch-3 space, turn.

Row 19: Ch 4, dc in first st, ch 4, skip next 3 dc, sc in next dc, ch 4, (dc, ch 1, dc) in top of turning ch. Fasten off.

Size L Only

Row 17: Ch 2, [sc in next ch-3 space, ch 3, sc in next ch-4 space, ch 5, sc in next ch-4 space, ch 3] twice, sc in ch-1 space, turn.

Row 18: Ch 2, sc in next ch-3 space, ch 1, 7 dc in next ch-5 space, ch 1, sc in next ch-3 space, ch 5, sc in next ch-3 space, ch 1, 7 dc in next ch-5 space, ch 1, sc in next ch-3 space, sc in top of turning ch, turn.

Row 19: Ch 4, dc in first st, ch 4, skip next 3 dc, sc in next dc, ch 4, V-st in next ch-5 space, ch 4, skip next 3 dc, sc in next dc, ch 4, V-st in last sc, turn.

Rows 20–22: repeat rows 17–19 once. Fasten off.

Size M Only

Row 1: With RS facing, join yarn in 4th dc of center 7 dc group (already holding last st of Row 1 of left front), ch 5, V-st in next ch-5 space, [ch 4, skip next 3 dc, sc in next dc, ch 4, V-st in next ch-5 space] twice, ch 4, skip next 3 dc, sc in next dc, ch 4, (dc, ch 1, dc) in last sc, turn.

Row 2: Ch 2, sc in next ch-1 space, [ch 3, sc in next ch-4 space, ch 5, sc in next ch-4 space, ch 3, sc in next ch-3 space] 3 times, ch 1, dc in top of turning ch, turn.

Row 3: Ch 2, sc in next ch-3 space, [ch 1, 7 dc in next ch-5 space, ch 1, sc in next ch-3 space, ch 5, sc in next ch-3 space] 3 times, sc in top of ch-2 turning ch, turn.

Row 4: Ch 4, dc in first st, [ch 4, skip next 3 dc, sc in next st, ch 4, V-st in next ch-5 space] twice, ch 4, skip next 3 dc, sc in next dc, ch 4, dc in last sc, turn.

Row 5: Ch 2, sc in next ch-4 space, [ch 5, sc in next ch-4 space, ch 3, sc in next ch-3 space, ch 3, sc in next ch-4 space] twice, ch 5, sc in next ch-4 space, ch 3, sc in next ch-1 space, sc in 3rd ch of ch-4 turning ch, turn.

Row 6: Ch 2, [sc in next ch-3 space, ch 1, 7 dc in next ch-5 space, ch 1, sc in next ch-3 space, ch 5] twice, sc in next ch-3 space, ch 1, 5 dc in next ch-5 space, dc2tog, working in same ch-5 space and in top of turning ch, turn.

Row 7: Ch 2, skip first 2 sts, sc in next st, [ch 4, V-st in next ch-5 space, ch 4, skip next 3 dc, sc in next dc] twice, ch 4, (dc, ch 1, dc) in last sc, turn.

Row 8: Ch 2, sc in next ch-1 space, [ch 3, sc in next ch-4 space, ch 5, sc in next ch-4 space, ch 3, sc in next ch-3 space] twice, ch 3, sc in next ch-4 space, ch 2, dc in top of turning ch, turn.

Row 9: Ch 3, 2 dc in next ch-2 space, ch 1, [sc in next ch-3 space, ch 5, sc in next ch-3 space, ch 1, 7 dc in next ch-5 space, ch 1] twice, sc in next ch-1 space, sc in 3rd ch of ch-4 turning ch, turn.

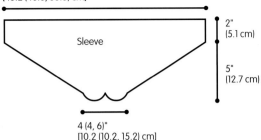

17 (19, 21)"
[43.2 (48.3, 53.3) cm]

Sleeve

2"
(5.1 cm)

5"
(12.7 cm)

4 (4, 6)"
[10.2 (10.2, 15.2) cm]

Row 10: Ch 4, dc in first st, [ch 4, skip next 3 dc, sc in next dc, ch 4, V-st in next ch-5 space] twice, skip next 2 dc, tr in top of turning ch, turn.

Row 11: Ch 2, [sc in next ch-3 space, ch 3, sc in next ch-4 space, ch 5, sc in next ch-4 space, ch 3] twice, sc in next ch-1 space, sc in 3rd ch of ch-4 turning ch, turn.

Row 12: Ch 2, sc in next ch-3 space, ch 1, 7 dc in next ch-5 space, ch 1, sc in next ch-3 space, ch 5, sc in next ch-3 space, ch 1, 7 dc in next ch-5 space, ch 1, sc in next ch-3 space, ch 1, dc in top of turning ch, turn.

Row 13: Ch 7, skip next 3 dc, sc in next dc, ch 4, V-st in next ch-5 space, ch 4, skip next 3 dc, sc in next dc, ch 4, (dc, ch 1, dc) in last sc, turn.

Row 14: Ch 2, sc in next ch-1 space, ch 3, sc in next ch-4 space, ch 5, sc in next ch-4 space, ch 3, sc in next ch-3 space, ch 3, sc in next ch-4 space, ch 5, 2 sc in last ch-7 space, turn.

Row 15: Ch 1, sc in first st, ch 1, 7 dc in next ch-5 space, ch 1, sc in next ch-3 space, ch 5, sc in next ch-3 space, ch 1, 7 dc in next ch-5 space, ch 1, sc in next ch-3 space, sc in last sc, turn.

Row 16: Ch 4, dc in first st, ch 4, skip next 3 dc, sc in next dc, ch 4, V-st in next ch-5 space, ch 4, skip next 3 dc, sc in next dc, ch 1, dc in last sc, turn.

Row 17: Ch 1, sc in next ch-1 space, ch 5, sc in next ch-4 space, ch 3, sc in next ch-3 space, ch 3, sc in next ch-4 space, ch 5, sc in next ch-4 space, ch 3, sc in next ch-1 space, sc in last sc, turn.

Row 18: Ch 2, sc in next ch-3 space, ch 1, 7 dc in next ch-5 space, ch 1, sc in next ch-3 space, ch 5, sc in next ch-3 space, ch 1, 4 dc in ch-5 space, dc2tog, working in same ch-5 space and in last sc, turn.

Row 19: Ch 2, skip first st, sc in next st, ch 4, V-st in next ch-5 space, ch 4, skip next 3 dc, sc in next dc, ch 4, (dc, ch 1, dc) in last sc, turn. Fasten off.

Sleeve

(Make 2)

Ch 23 (23, 35)

Row 1: Sc in 2nd ch and in each of next ch across, turn. (22 [22, 34] sc)

Row 2 (WS): Ch 5, skip first st, [FPtr10tog in next 10 sts, ch 6, sc in next st] 2 (2, 3) times, turn. (2 [2, 3] clusters)

Row 3 (extended row): Ch 16 (loosely) (counts as dtr, ch 12 for next cluster), sc in 2nd ch from hook and in each of next 9 ch sts (forms first cluster), skip 5 ch (for dtr) and next sc, *dtr in next ch, tr in next ch, dc in next ch, hdc in next ch, sc in next ch, skip next ch and next cluster, sc in next ch, hdc in next ch, dc in next ch, tr in next ch, dtr in next ch*, ch 1, skip next sc, rep from * to * once, dtr in last st, work extended Fsc as follows: ch 1, insert hook in top of dtr just made, yo, draw through 1 loop, yo, and draw through 2 loops (first Fsc made), work 10 Fsc (forms last cluster), turn. (4 clusters)

Row 4: Skip first st, ch 5, FPtr10tog in next 10 sts, ch 6, sc in first dtr, *ch 5, FPtr10tog in next 10 sts, ch 6*, sc in ch-1 space; rep from * to * once, sc in 5th ch of ch-16 of previous row, ch 5, FPtr10tog in next 10 sts, ch 6, sc in top of turning ch, turn.

Row 5 (extended row): Ch 16 (loosely) (counts as dtr, ch 12 for next cluster), sc in 2nd ch from hook and in each of next 9 ch sts (forms first cluster), skip 5 ch (for dtr) and next sc, *dtr in next ch, tr in next ch, dc in next ch, hdc in next ch, sc in next ch, skip next ch and next cluster, sc in next ch, hdc in next ch, dc in next ch, tr in next ch, dtr in next ch**, ch 1, skip next sc; rep from * across, ending last rep at **, dtr in last st, work first extended Fsc as before, work 10 Fsc (for last cluster), turn. (6 clusters)

Row 6: Skip first st, ch 5, FPtr10tog in next 10 sts, ch 6, sc in first dtr, *ch 5, FPtr10tog in next 10 sts, ch 6**, sc in ch-1 space; rep from * across, ending last repeat before extension at **, sc in 5th ch of ch-16 of previous row, ch 5, FPtr10tog in next 10 sts, ch 6, sc in top of turning ch, turn. (6 clusters)

Rows 7 and 8: Rep Rows 5-6 once. (8 [8, 9] clusters)

Rows 9, 10 (11, 12): Work straight without extensions.

Fasten off.

Finishing

Sew shoulder seams. Sew side seams. Fold sleeves in half lengthwise. Matching fold to shoulder seam, pin straight sides of one sleeve to horizontal parts of the armhole, and sew the sleeve in place. Work the same way for the other sleeve.

Neck Trim

Rnd 1: With RS facing, join yarn on neck edge at left shoulder seam, ch 1, *work 2 sc in each row* of the front neck down to center 3 sts, then work sc3tog in center, rep from * to * up other side of next shaping, 3 sc in each ch-4 and ch-3 space across back neck, join with Sl st in first sc. Fasten off.

Blocking

Lay garment flat on a padded surface. Spray with water and pat into shape. Allow to dry. Do not iron.

Skill Level

Intermediate

Yarn

Classic Elite Wool Bam Boo; 50%
wool, 50% bamboo viscose; 118
yd (108 m)/1.75oz (50 g); #1658
Tomato: 9 (10, 11) skeins

qipao tunic

I love Asian fashion. From Tokyo to
New Delhi, the styles and colors
are beautiful to look at and wear.
This piece is a Qipao, pronounced
shee'Pow. The Qipao is a traditional
Chinese dress that became very
popular in the 1920s and has gone on
to become an iconic look for an entire
culture. For my interpretation of this
classic I decided to use a bright red
yarn in a flat stitch. I added the spike
stitches as homage to the embroidery
you might find on an original Qipao.
The frog closures are the perfect
finishing touch to this Chinese classic.

Designed by
Shannon
Mullett-Bowlsby

Hook

5/F (3.75 mm)

Gauge

21 sts = 4" (10cm); 20 rows = 4 ¼" (11cm) in pattern.

Notions

Five frog closures

Yarn needle

Finished Sizes

Women's sizes S (M, L)

To fit bust size: 32 (36, 40)" (81.5 [91.5, 101.5] cm)

Finished bust: 34 (38, 42)" (86.5 [96.5, 106.5] cm)

Finished length: 28 (28 ¼, 28½)" (71 [72, 72] cm)

Reduced Sample of Pattern

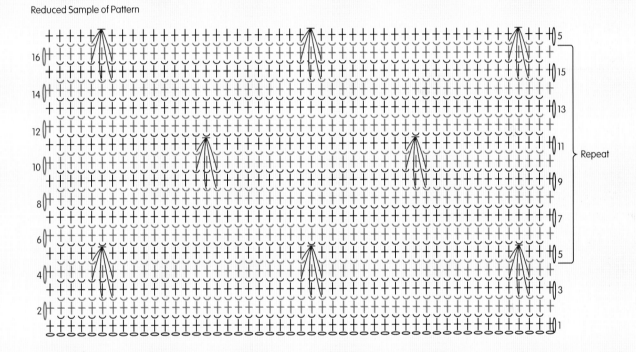

Notes

1. When instructed to work into a stitch 4 rows below, insert the hook in a stitch in the row numbered 4 less than the row you are working. For example, if you are working Row 5, a stitch "4 rows" below is in Row 5 – 4 = Row 1.

2. When instructed to "work in pattern as established", continue to work in the pattern of 5 rows of sc in front loop only followed by 1 row that includes 5-Spikes. Take care to work the first and last stitch of each row under both loops (not in the in front loop only), and ensure that the 5-spikes are centered between the 5-spikes of the previous spike row.

Special Stitches

Foundation single crochet (fsc): *Start with a slip knot, ch 2, insert hook in 2nd ch from hook, draw up a loop, yo, draw through 1 loop, yo, and draw through 2 loops—1 single crochet with its own chain at bottom. Work next stitch under loops of that chain. Insert hook under 2 loops at bottom of the previous stitch, draw up a loop, yo and draw through 1 loop, yo and draw through 2 loops. Repeat for length of foundation.*

5-spike: *Insert hook in previous stitch (to the right of the hook) 2 rows below and draw up a loop, insert hook in same stitch 3 rows below and draw up a loop, insert hook in next stitch (directly below hook) 4 rows below, insert hook in next stitch (to the left of hook) 3 rows below, insert hook in same stitch 2 rows below, yarn over and draw through all 6 loops on hook. Notes: Skip the corresponding stitch of the current row (it should be covered by the 5-spike). If you are left-handed begin by inserting the hook in the previous stitch (to the LEFT of the hook) 2 rows below.*

Front

Row 1: Fsc 90 (100, 110) sts, turn.

Rows 2–4: Ch 1, sc in first st, sc in front loop only of each st across to last st, sc in last st, turn.

Row 5 (spike row 1): Ch 1, sc in first st, sc in front loop only of next 4 (9, 4) sts, 5-spike in next st, [sc in front loop only of next 19 sts, 5-spike in next st] 4 (4, 5) times, sc in front loop only of next 3 (8, 3) sts, sc in last st, turn.

Rows 6–10: Ch 1, sc in first st, sc in front loop only of each st across to last st, sc in last st, turn.

Row 11 (spike row 2): Ch 1, sc in first st, sc in front loop only of next 14 (19, 14) sts, 5-spike in next st, [sc in front loop only of next 19 sts, 5-spike in next st] 3 (3, 4) times, sc in front loop only of next 13 (18, 13) sts, sc in last st, turn.

Rows 12–16: Ch 1, sc in first st, sc in front loop only of each st across to last st, sc in last st, turn.

Repeat Rows 5–16 until piece measures about 21 (20¾, 20½)" (53.5 [52.5, 52] cm) from beginning.

Shape Armholes

Row 1: Sl st in first 5 sts, ch 1, sc in next st, work in pattern as established to last 6 sts, sc in next st, turn, leaving last 5 sts unworked. (80 [90, 100] sts)

Rows 2–7 (9, 12): Ch 1, sc in first st, sc2tog, work in pattern as established to last 3 sts, sc2tog, sc in last st, turn. (68 [74, 78] sts at the end of last row)

Work even in pattern as established until armhole measures 3½ (4, 4½)" (9 [10, 11.5] cm).

Divide for Neck

First Side of Front Neck Split

Row 1: Ch 1, sc in first st, work in pattern as established across next 32 (35, 37) sts, sc in next st, turn, leaving remaining sts unworked for 2nd side of front neck split. (34 [37, 39] sts)

Work even in pattern as established until armhole measures 7 (7½, 8)" (18 [19, 20.5] cm). Fasten off.

Second Side of Front Neck Split

Row 1: Join yarn with sc in first unworked st following first side of front neck split, work in pattern as established across remaining unworked sts to last st, sc in last st, turn. (34 [37, 39] sts)

Work even in pattern as established until 2nd side measures same as first side. Fasten off.

Back

Work same as front to armhole shaping.

Shape Armholes

Row 1: Sl st in first 5 sts, ch 1, sc in next st, work in pattern as established to last 6 sts, sc in next st, turn, leaving last 5 sts unworked. (80 [90, 100] sts)

Rows 2–7 (9, 12): Ch 1, sc in first st, sc2tog, work in pattern as established to last 3 sts, sc2tog, sc in last st, turn. (68 [74, 78] sts at the end of last row)

Work even in pattern as established until armhole measures 7 (7½, 8)" (18 [19, 20.5] cm). Fasten off.

Finishing

Beginning at armhole edges, sew shoulder seams for 2 (2½, 3)" (5 [6.5, 7.5] cm).

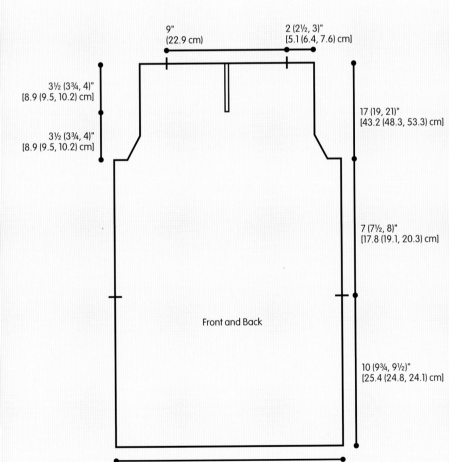

9"
(22.9 cm)

2 (2½, 3)"
[5.1 (6.4, 7.6) cm]

3½ (3¾, 4)"
[8.9 (9.5, 10.2) cm]

3½ (3¾, 4)"
[8.9 (9.5, 10.2) cm]

17 (19, 21)"
[43.2 (48.3, 53.3) cm]

7 (7½, 8)"
[17.8 (19.1, 20.3) cm]

Front and Back

10 (9¾, 9½)"
[25.4 (24.8, 24.1) cm]

11"
(27.9 cm)

Collar

With RS facing, join yarn in front corner (at top of neck split), to work around neck edge.

Row 1: Ch 1, sc evenly spaced around neck edge to opposite front corner, taking care to work 1 sc in each shoulder seam, turn.

Row 2: Ch 1, sc in both loops of first st, sc in front loop only of each st across to last st, sc in both loops of last st, turn.

Repeat Row 2 until collar measures about 2" (5 cm), ending with a WS row.

Last row (RS): Ch 1, turn, sc in both loops of each st across, do not turn, sc evenly down side edge of collar and edge of neck split, sc evenly up other side edge of neck split and side edge of collar; join with Sl st in first sc. Fasten off.

Prepare side edges: With RS facing, join yarn with sc at beginning of one side edge of front, sc evenly across side edge. Fasten off. Repeat across other side edge of front and side edges of back.

Beginning at underarms, sew side seams for 10 (9 ¾, 9½)" (25.5 [25, 24] cm), leaving 11" (28 cm) open for side slit.

Armhole edging: With RS facing, join yarn with sc in armhole edge at under-arm, sc evenly spaced around armhole edge, join with Sl st in first sc. Fasten off. Repeat edging around other armhole.

Finishing

Sew one frog closure, centered over front neck split. Sew two frog closures, evenly spaced over each side slit. Weave in ends.

dresses and skirts

Skill Level
Experienced.

Yarn
Blue Heron Egyptian Cotton; 100%
cotton, 1000 yds (914.5 m)/8 oz
(227 g); color corn: 3 (3, 4) skeins

fiesta convertible skirt and shell

Designed by
Margaret Hubert

I envisioned this skirt and sketched it long
before I was sure just how I was going
to "make it work". The answer came to
me in one of my middle-of-the-night
thoughts. The unusual construction of this
skirt gives you two skirts in one. Wear it
as a short pencil skirt, or slip on the ruffly
flounce which is attached to a half slip to
convert to a long, elegant party skirt. Pair
the skirt with the Fiesta Shell to complete
the outfit. The yarn used is 100% cotton,
with a beautiful sheen, easy to crochet
with, easy to wear.

Hooks

3/D (3.25 mm)
4/E (3.5 mm)
5/F (3.75 mm)
6/G (4 mm)

Gauge

24 sts = 4" (10 cm) with 3/D (3.25 mm) hook

2 repeats and 6 rows in triple loop pattern = 4" (10 cm)

Notions

Tapestry needle
Yarn needle
Half slip (sample was made with Slimplicity by Spanx, available on line at: http://www.spanx.com

Finished Sizes

Women's sizes S (M, L)
Finished waist: 33 (34, 35)" (84 [86.5, 89] cm)
Finished hip: 36 (38, 40)" (91.5 [96.5, 101.5] cm)
Pencil skirt length: 20 (20½, 21)" (51 [52, 53.5] cm)
Bottom flounce length: 18 (18½, 19)" (45.5 [47, 48.5] cm)

Notes

Skirt is worked in the round starting at waist; mark joining as side seam.

Special Stitches

V-st: *(Dc, ch 3, dc) in same st or space.*

Small shell: *(2 dc, ch 2, 2 dc) in same st or space.*

Large shell: *(3 dc, ch 3, 3 dc) in same st or space.*

Triple Loop Pattern

Rnd 1: *Ch 7 (counts as dc, ch 4), skip next 4 sc, *(sc, ch 7, sc , ch 7, sc, ch 7, sc) in next sc**, ch 4, skip next 4 sc, dc in next sc, ch 4, skip next 4 sc; rep from * around, ending last rep at **, ch 4, join with Sl st in the 3rd ch of the beg ch 7.*

Rnd 2: *Ch 1, sc in first st, *ch 1, sc in next ch-7 loop, [ch 3, 1 sc in next ch-7 loop] twice, ch 1,** 1 sc in next dc , rep from * around, ending last rep at **, join with Sl st in first sc.*

Rnd 3: *Ch 1, sc in first st, ch 7, sc in the first dc, *ch 4, skip next sc, dc in next ch-7 loop, ch 4, skip next sc**, (sc, ch 7, sc, ch 7, sc, ch 7, sc) in next sc; rep from * around, ending last repeat at **, (sc, ch 3, sc) in first sc, ch 3, tr in first forming center ch-7 loop.*

Rnd 4: *Ch 1, sc in first loop, ch 3, sc in the next ch-7 loop, *ch 1, sc in next dc**, ch 1, sc in next ch-7 loop, [ch 3, sc in next ch-7 loop] twice; rep from * around, ending last repeat at **, ch 1, sc in next ch-7 loop, ch 3, join with Sl st in first sc.*

Rnd 5: *Ch 1, (sc, ch 7, sc, ch 7, sc, ch 7, sc) in first sc, *ch 4, skip next sc, dc in next sc, ch 4, skip next sc**, (sc, ch 7, sc, ch 7, sc, ch 7, sc) in next sc; rep from * around, ending last repeat at **, join with Sl st in first sc.*

Rep Rows 2–5 for pattern.

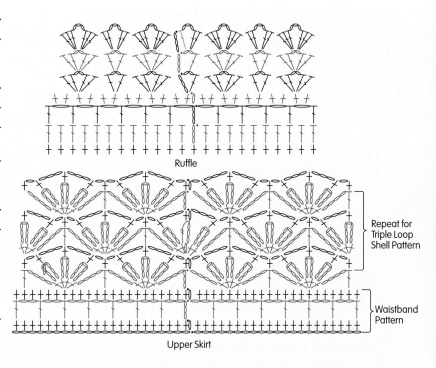

Ruffle

Repeat for Triple Loop Shell Pattern

Waistband Pattern

Upper Skirt

Pencil Skirt

Waistband

With 3/D hook, ch 198 (204, 210) and being careful not to twist ch, join with Sl st in first ch to form a ring.

Rnd 1: Ch 1, sc in each ch around, join with Sl st in first sc.

Rnd 2: Ch 5 (counts as dc, ch 2), skip next 2 sc, *dc in next sc, ch 2, skip next 2 sc; rep from * around, join with a sl st to 3rd ch of beg ch-5. (66 [68, 70] dc and ch-2 spaces)

Size S Only

Rnd 3: Ch 1, sc in first st, *2 sc in next ch-2 space, sc in next dc, rep from * around, ending with 3 sc in last space. (200 sc)

Size M Only

Rnd 3: Ch 1, sc in first st, *[2 sc in next ch-2 space, sc in next dc] 10 times, 2 sc in next ch-2 space, 2 sc in next dc (inc made); rep from * 6 times, join with Sl st in first sc. (210 sc)

Size L Only

Rnd 3: Ch 1, 2 sc in first st (inc made), *[2 sc in next ch-2 space, sc in next dc] 6 times, 2 sc in next ch-2 space**, 2 sc in next dc (inc made), rep from * 9 times, ending last rep at **, join with Sl st in first sc. (220 sc)

All Sizes

Still using the 3/D hook, work even in triple loop pattern on 20 (21, 22) loop shells for 5" (12.5 cm). Change to 5/F hook. Work even in triple loop pattern for 5" (12.5 cm). Change to 6/G hook. Work even in triple loop pattern until piece measures 17½ (18, 18½)" (44.5 [45.5, 47] cm) from beg, ending with Rnd 2 of pattern.

Bottom Border Ruffle

Rnd 1: With 6/G hook, ch 1, sc in first st, sc evenly around, working sc in each st, sc in each ch-1 space, 3 dc in each ch-3 space around, join with Sl st in first sc. (240 [252, 264] sc)

Rnd 2: Ch 3 (counts as dc), skip first sc, dc in each sc around, join with Sl st in top of beg ch-3.

Rnd 3: Ch 4 (counts as dc, ch 1), skip next dc, *dc in next dc, ch 1, skip next dc; rep from * around, join with Sl st in 3rd ch of beg ch-4. (120 [126, 132] ch-1 spaces)

Rnd 4: Ch 1, 2 sc in each ch-1 space around, join with Sl st in first sc. (240 [252, 264] sc)

Rnd 5: Ch 3 (counts as half V-st here and throughout), *skip next 2 sc, small shell in next sc, skip next 2 sc, V-st in next sc; rep from * around, ending with dc in first sc, ch 2, join with Sl st in 3rd ch of beg ch-3 to complete V-st.

Rnd 6: Ch 3, (counts as half V-st), *small shell in ch-2 space of next shell, V-st in ch-2 space of next V-st; rep from * around, ending with dc in last ch-2 space, ch 2, join with Sl st in 3rd ch of beg ch-3 to complete V-st.

Rnd 7: Ch 3 (counts as dc), *large shell in ch-2 space of next shell, small shell in ch-2 space of next V-st; rep from * around, ending with (2 dc, ch 2, dc) in the last ch-2 space to complete last small shell, join with Sl st in top of beg ch-3. Fasten off.

Waist Tie

With 6/G hook and 3 strands of yarn held together as one, ch 225. Fasten off. Weave tie in and out of ch-2 spaces at waist.

This completes pencil skirt or top part of full skirt.

Bottom Flounce

Note: *First tier is worked with 5/F (3.75 mm) hook; last two tiers are worked with 6/G (4 mm) hook.*

Preparing Slip

Starting at one side seam, using a needle threaded with yarn, working in blanket stitch across bottom edge of slip, work 65 (67, 69) evenly spaced blanket stitches on one side of slip, work 65 (68, 70) evenly spaced blanket stitches on other side of slip. (130 [135, 139] sts)

First Tier

Rnd 1: With 5/F hook join yarn in first blanket st to left of side seam on slip, ch 3 (counts as dc), 2 (1, 2) dc in first blanket st, 2 dc in each blanket st around, join with Sl st in top of beg ch-3. (261 [270, 279] dc)

Rnd 2: Ch 5 (counts as dc, ch 2), skip next 2 dc, *dc in next dc, ch 2, skip next 2 dc; rep from * around, join with Sl st in 3rd ch of beg ch-5. (87 [90, 93] ch-2 spaces)

Rnd 3: Ch 1, sc in first st, 1 (2, 3) sc in next ch-2 space, *sc in next dc, 2 sc in next ch-2 space; rep from * around. (260 [270, 280] sc)

Work even in triple loop pattern on 26 (27, 28) loop shells for 5" (12.5 cm) ending with Rnd 2 or Rnd 4 of pattern.

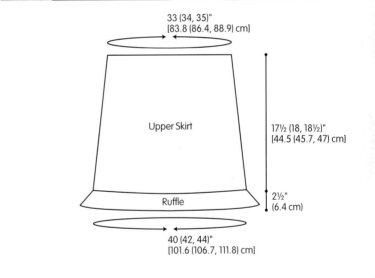

33 (34, 35)" [83.8 (86.4, 88.9) cm]

Upper Skirt

17½ (18, 18½)" [44.5 (45.7, 47) cm]

Ruffle

2½" (6.4 cm)

40 (42, 44)" [101.6 (106.7, 111.8) cm]

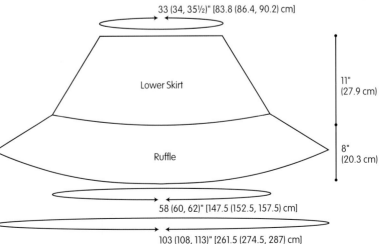

33 (34, 35½)" [83.8 (86.4, 90.2) cm]

Lower Skirt

11" (27.9 cm)

Ruffle

8" (20.3 cm)

58 (60, 62)" [147.5 (152.5, 157.5) cm]

103 (108, 113)" [261.5 (274.5, 287) cm]

Yarn

Blue Heron Egyptian Cotton;
100% cotton; 1000 yds (91.5 m)/8
oz (227 g); color peach: 3 (3, 4)
skeins

Second Tier

Rnd 1: With 6/G hook, ch 1, *sc in next ch-1 space, sc in next sc, 3 sc in next ch-3 space, sc in next sc, 3 sc in next ch-3 space, sc in next sc, sc in next ch-1 space, skip the next sc; rep from * around, join with Sl st in first sc. (286 [297, 308] sc)

Rnd 2: Ch 3, work in dc, inc 4 (3, 2) dc, evenly spaced around, join with Sl st in first sc. (290 [300, 310] dc)

Rnd 3: Ch 4 (counts as a dc, ch 1), skip first dc, dc in next dc, *ch 1, skip next dc, dc in next dc; rep from * around, ending with ch 1, join with Sl st to 3rd ch of the beg ch-4. (145 [150, 155] ch-1 spaces)

Rnd 4: Ch 1, 2 sc in each ch-1 space around, join with Sl st in first sc. (290 [300, 310] sc)

Work even in triple loop pattern on 29 (30, 31) loop shells for 5" more.

Third Tier

Rnd 1: With 6/G hook, ch 1, sc in first sc, *sc in next ch-1 space, sc in next sc, 3 sc in the next ch-3 space, sc in next sc, 3 sc in next ch-3 space, sc in next sc, sc in next ch-1 space, sc in the next sc; rep from * around, join with Sl st in first sc. (348 [360, 372] sc)

Rnd 2: Ch 3 (count as dc), skip first sc, dc in each sc around, join with Sl st in top of beg ch-3.

Rnd 3: Ch 4 (counts as a dc, ch 1), skip next dc, *dc in next dc, ch 1, skip next dc; rep from * around, join with Sl st to 3rd ch of the beg ch-4. (174 [180, 186] ch-1 spaces)

Rnd 4: Ch 1, 2 sc in each ch-1 space around, join with Sl st in first sc. (348 [360, 372] sc).

Rnd 5: Ch 3, *skip next 2 sc, small shell in next sc, skip next 2 sc, V-st in next sc; rep from * around, ending with dc in first sc, ch 2, join with Sl st in 3rd ch of beg ch-3 to complete V-st. (58 [60, 62] shells and V sts)

Rnd 6: Ch 3, *small shell in ch-2 sp of next shell, V-st in ch-2 space of next V-st; rep from * around, ending with dc in last ch-2 space, ch 2, join with Sl st in 3rd ch of beg ch-3 to complete V-st.

Rnds 7–10: Rep Rnd 6.

Rnds 11–16: Ch 3, *large shell in ch-2 space of next shell, V-st in ch-2 space of next V-st; rep from * around, ending with 1 dc in ch-2 space of last V-st, ch 2, join with a sl st to top of beg ch-3.

Rnd 17: Ch 3, dc in same st as beg ch-3, *large shell in ch-3 space of next shell, small shell in ch-2 space of next V-st; rep from * around, ending with 2 dc in ch-2 space of last V-st, ch 3, join with Sl st in top of beg ch-3. Fasten off.

Finishing

Weave in ends. Lay garment flat on a padded surface, sprinkle with water, using rust proof pins, pin into shape, allow to dry.

Hooks

5/F (3.75 mm)

6/G (4 mm)

Gauge

With 6/G (4 mm) hook, 16 sts and 14 rows hdc = 4" (10 cm).

Notions

Yarn needle

Stitch marker

Finished Sizes

Women's sizes S (M, L, XL)

Finished bust: 32 (34, 36, 38)" (81.5 [86.5, 91.5, 96.5] cm)

Finished length: 18½ (19½, 20½, 21½)" (47 [49.5, 52, 54.5] cm)

This is a very close fitting garment. Fabric is very stretchy and hugs the body.

Note

Garment starts at waistline and worked to shoulders. Bottom trim is added later.

Special Stitches

Hdc2tog: *[Yo, insert hook in next st, yo, draw yarn through st] twice, yo, draw yarn through all loops on hook.*

V-st: *(Dc, ch 2, dc) in same st or space.*

Small shell: *(2 dc, ch 2, 2 dc) in same st or space.*

Large shell: *(3 dc, ch 3, 3 dc) in same st or space.*

Back

With 6/G (4 mm) hook, ch 65 (71, 77, 83).

Foundation Row: Sc in 2nd ch from hook, sc in each ch across, turn. (64 [70, 76, 82] sc)

Row 1 (RS): Ch 2 (counts as hdc here and throughout), skip first st, hdc in each st across, turn. (64 [70, 76, 82] hdc)

Rep Row 1 until piece measures 8 (8½, 9, 9½)" (20.5 [21.5, 23, 24] cm) from beg.

Shape Armholes

Next Row: Sl st over first 4 (4, 5, 5) sts, ch 2, work in hdc across to within last 4 (4, 5, 5) sts of other side, turn, leaving remaining st unworked. (56 [62, 66, 72] hdc)

Next Row: Ch 2, skip first st, hdc2tog (dec), hdc in each st across to last 3 sts, hdc2tog (dec), hdc in top of turning ch, turn. (54 [60, 64, 70] hdc)

In same manner, work in hdc, dec 1 st at each end of every row (3 times). (48 [54, 58, 64] hdc at end of last row)

Work even on 48 (54, 58, 64) sts until armhole measures 5½ (6, 6½, 7)" (14 [15, 16.5, 18] cm) from beg of shaping, ending with a wrong side row, turn.

Right Back

Next Row: Ch 2, skip first st, hdc in next 10 (10, 11, 11) sts, turn, leaving remaining sts unworked.

Work in hdc, dec 1 st at neck edge, every row (7 times). Work even on remaining 4 (4, 5, 5) sts until armhole measures 8 (8½, 9, 9½)" from beg of shaping. Fasten off.

Left Back

Next Row: Skip 26 (32, 34, 40) center sts, join yarn in next st, ch 2, hdc in each of last 10 (10, 11, 11) sts, turn.

Work in hdc, dec 1 st at neck edge, every row (7 times). Work even on remaining 4 (4, 5, 5) sts until armhole measures same as left front. Fasten off.

Front

Work same as back until armhole measures 2½ (3, 3½, 4)" from beg of armhole shaping.

Left Front

Work same as right back.

Right Front

Work same as left back.

Finishing

Sew shoulder seams. Sew underarm seams.

Armhole Border

Place a marker centered between underarm and shoulder on each side of armhole opening.

With 5/F hook, join yarn with Sl st at underarm, ch 1, work 21 (22, 23, 24) sc evenly spaced to first marker, work 21 (22, 23, 24) sc evenly spaced to shoulder seam, work 21 (22, 23, 24) sc evenly spaced to next marker, work 21 (22, 23, 24) sc evenly spaced to underarm, join with Sl st in first sc. (84 [88, 92, 96] sc)

Rnd 2: Ch 5 (counts as a dc, ch 2), skip next sc, *dc in next sc, ch 2, skip next sc; rep from * around, join with Sl st to 3rd ch of beg ch-5. (42 [44, 46, 48] ch-2 spaces)

Rnd 3: Ch 1, 2 sc in each ch-2 space around, join with Sl st in first sc. Fasten off. (84 [88, 92, 96] sc)

Neck Border

Rnd 1: With 5/F hook, join yarn with Sl st at right shoulder seam, ch 1, work 17 (18, 19, 20) sc evenly spaced across right back neck shaping, work 1 sc in each of the next 26 (32, 34, 40) hdc, work 17 (18, 19, 20) sc evenly spaced across left back neck shaping to shoulder seam, work 25 (26, 27, 28) sc evenly spaced across left front neck shaping, 1 sc in each of the next 26 (32, 34, 40) hdc, work 25 (26, 27, 28) sc evenly spaced across right front neck shaping, join with Sl st in first sc. (136 [152, 162, 178] sc)

Rnd 2: Ch 5 (counts as a dc, ch2), skip next sc, *dc in next sc, ch 2, skip next sc; rep from * around, join with Sl st to the 3rd ch of beg ch-5. (68 [76, 81, 89] ch-2 spaces)

Rnd 3: Ch 1, 2 sc in each ch-2 space around, join with Sl st in first sc. Fasten off. (136 [152, 162, 178] sc)

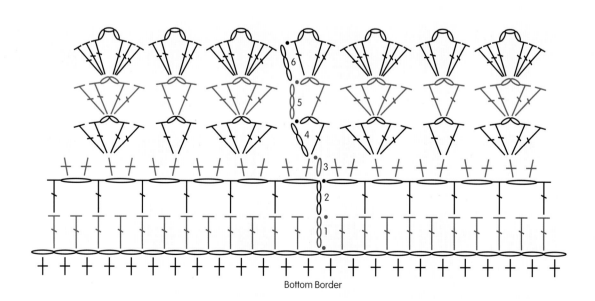

Bottom Border

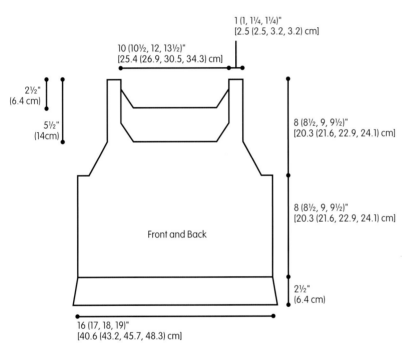

1 (1, 1¼, 1¼)"
[2.5 (2.5, 3.2, 3.2) cm]

10 (10½, 12, 13½)"
[25.4 (26.9, 30.5, 34.3) cm]

2½"
(6.4 cm)

5½"
(14cm)

8 (8½, 9, 9½)"
[20.3 (21.6, 22.9, 24.1) cm]

Front and Back

8 (8½, 9, 9½)"
[20.3 (21.6, 22.9, 24.1) cm]

2½"
(6.4 cm)

16 (17, 18, 19)"
[40.6 (43.2, 45.7, 48.3) cm]

Bottom Border

Work on other side of beginning ch, using the 6 or G hook.

Rnd 1: With RS facing, using 6/G hook, working across bottom edge of garment, between sts in Row 1, join yarn with Sl st between any 2 sc in Row 1, ch 3 (counts as dc), dc in each space between 2 sc in Row 1 around bottom edge, skipping the seam sts, join with Sl st in top of beg ch-3. (126 [138, 150, 164] dc)

Rnd 2: Ch 5 (counts as dc, ch 2), skip next dc, *dc in next dc, ch 2, skip next dc; rep from * around, join with Sl st in 3rd ch of beg ch-5. (63 [69, 75, 82] ch-2 spaces)

Rnd 3: Ch 1, 2 sc in each ch-2 space around. (126 [138, 150, 164] sc)

Rnd 4: Ch 3 (counts as half V-st), *skip next 2 sc, small shell in next sc, skip 2 sc, V-st in next sc; rep from * around, ending with dc in first sc, ch 2, join with Sl st in 3rd ch of beg ch-3 to complete V-st. (21 [23, 25, 27] shell sts and V-sts)

Rnd 5: Ch 3, (counts as half V-st), *small shell in next ch-2 space, V-st in next ch-2 space; rep from * around, ending with dc in first sc, ch 2, join with Sl st in 3rd ch of beg ch-3 to complete V-st.

Rnd 6: Ch 3 (counts as dc), *large shell in ch-2 space of next shell, small shell in ch-2 space of next V-st; rep from * around, ending with (2 dc, ch 2, dc) in the last ch-2 space to complete last small shell, join with Sl st in top of beg ch-3. Fasten off.

Blocking

Weave in ends. Lay garment flat on a padded surface, sprinkle with water, using rust proof pins, pin into shape, allow to dry.

Skill Level

Experienced

Yarn

(CYCA category 3 light)
Louisa Harding Mulberry; 100%
silk; 136 yd (124 m)/1 ¾ oz (50 g);
#4 Rose: 4 (4, 5, 5, 6) skeins for
skirt; 3 (4, 4, 5, 5) skeins for top

Hooks

7 (4.5 mm)

malahini two-piece dress

Designed by
Doris Chan

Pair this lacy duo for a fashion–forward dress that shows off your curves. The top is cropped and slightly fitted to above the waist, with a rounded ribbed collar, three-quarter length banded sleeves. The slim, straight skirt hits just above the knee and features a special softly elasticized waistband that lies beautifully flat and never pinches. Both pieces are virtually seamless and easily adjusted for length, even after the fact. The lace fabric is incredibly stretchy and offers an easy, comfortable fit beyond the finished measurements.

Gauge

6 Fsc = 4" (10 cm)

In shell stitch pattern, 3 reps = 5" (12.5 cm); 4 rnds = 2 ¾" (7 cm)

In Sl st ribbing of skirt (with carry–along elastic), 6 sts = 1" (2.5 cm); 17 rows = 4" (10 cm)

In Sl st ribbing of Top, 5 sts = ¾" (2 cm); 19 rows = 4" (10 cm)

Notions

Stitch markers

Tapestry needle

Rainbow Elastic (Bryson Distributing) 1 mm Fine; 50 yd (45m) per card; one card #83 light pink

Finished Sizes

Women's sizes XS (S, M, L, XL)

As finished and blocked:

Skirt:

Finished waist: 22½ (25½, 28, 31, 34)" (57 (65, 71, 79, 86.5) cm) with stretch to pull on

Finished full hips: 32½ (36, 39, 42, 45½)" (82.5 (91.5, 99, 106.5, 115.5) cm)

Finished length: 19" (48.5 cm)

Top:

Finished bust: 30 (33½, 36½, 40, 43½)" (76 (85, 92.5, 101.5, 110.5) cm)

Finished waist: 23½ (26½, 30, 33½, 36½)" (59.5 (67.5, 76, 85, 92.5] cm)

Finished length (from back neck including collar): 12 (13½, 14½, 14½, 16)" (30.5 (34.5, 37, 37.5, 40.5] cm)

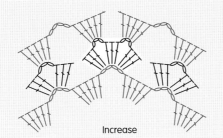

Increase

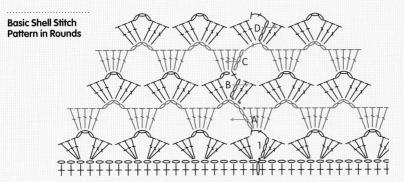

Basic Shell Stitch Pattern in Rounds

Notes

Both the skirt and top are crocheted seamlessly from the top down in joined rounds, worked back and forth, turned after every round. The ribbed waistband of the skirt and the ribbed collar of the top are made first. This has the advantage of giving you a better idea of the fit as you try on the garments as you go.

Special Stitches

Foundation single crochet (fsc): *Start with a slip knot, ch 2, insert hook in 2nd ch from hook, draw up a loop, yo, draw through 1 loop, yo, and draw through 2 loops—1 single crochet with its own chain at bottom. Work next stitch under loops of that chain. Insert hook under 2 loops at bottom of the previous stitch, draw up a loop, yo and draw through 1 loop, yo and draw through 2 loops. Repeat for length of foundation.*

Shell: *(3 dc, ch 3, 3 dc) in same st or space.*

V-st: *(dc, ch 3, dc) in same st or space.*

Basic Shell Stitch Pattern in Rounds

Pattern Rnd A (RS): *Ch 7 (counts as dc, ch 4), [5 dc in ch-3 space of next shell, ch 4] around, end with 4 dc in same space as beginning, Sl st in 3rd ch of beginning ch-7, Sl st in each of next 2 chs of beginning space, turn.*

Pattern Rnd B (WS): *Ch 3 (counts as dc), 2 dc in first space, shell in each ch-4 space around, end with 3 dc in same space as beginning, ch 2, sc in 3rd ch of beginning ch (counts as last ch-3 space), turn.*

Pattern Rnd C (RS): *Ch 3 (counts as dc), 4 dc in beginning space, [ch 4, 5 dc in ch-3 space of next shell] around, end with ch 1, dc in 3rd ch of beginning ch–7 (counts as last ch-4 space), turn.*

Pattern Rnd D (WS): *Ch 3 (equals dc), 2 dc in beginning space, shell in each ch-4 space around, end with 3 dc in same space as beginning, dc in 3rd ch of beginning ch (counts as last ch-3 space), turn.*

Skirt

Waistband

Foundation: Work 96 (108, 120, 132, 144) Fsc, Sl st in beg sc to form a ring, being careful not to twist foundation; do not turn, RS of sc edge still facing, begin work across sc of foundation.

Add one strand of elastic thread to the feeder yarn, holding strands together as one, begin ribbing, working one row of Sl st for each sc of foundation.

Row 1 (RS): Ch 7, do not turn.

Row 2 (RS): Rotate and work in RS face of chains just made, Sl st in 2nd ch from hook, Sl st in each ch across, turn. (6 Sl sts)

Row 3 (WS): With feed yarn now to the back of work as usual, moving backwards (left to right), Sl st in each of next 2 sc of foundation; now moving forwards (right to left) skip 2 Sl sts just made, Sl st in back loop of next 6 Sl sts, turn.

Row 4 (RS): Ch 1, skip ch-1 just made, Sl st in back loop of next 6 Sl sts, turn.

Rows 5–96 (108, 120, 132, 144): Rep Rows 3–4 around sc edge of foundation.

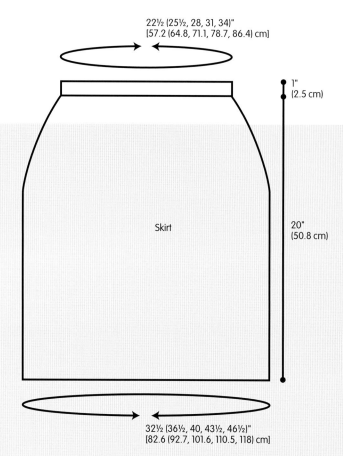

22½ (25½, 28, 31, 34)"
[57.2 (64.8, 71.1, 78.7, 86.4) cm]

1"
(2.5 cm)

Skirt

20"
(50.8 cm)

32½ (36½, 40, 43½, 46½)"
[82.6 (92.7, 101.6, 110.5, 118) cm]

Waistband Finishing

After last rep of Row 4, turn, Sl st in last remaining sc of foundation, Sl st in same sc as beginning. Fasten off, leaving a few inches of yarn for sewing short ribbing seam. Turn, on RS of waistband, drop elastic strand, thread yarn on a tapestry needle, matching 6 Sl st of last row with 6 spare loops of beginning ch, working back and forth, taking one strand of edge for each stitch, working in mattress stitch, sew last row to base of foundation. Fasten off. Weave in ends.

Skirt Body

With WS of foundation facing, chain edge now on top, join yarn with Sl st in chain corresponding to the first row of ribbed band, now the center back of skirt.

Work 16 (18, 20, 22, 24) shell stitch repeats around foundation, using 6 foundation sts per repeat.

Note: *The nicest location for the joining of rounds is at or near the center back of skirt. The join wanders one half rep off the exact center back, and then bounces back again as you work the pattern rounds. Keeping track of this location will help you remember where you are in the progression of pattern rounds, so you may wish to mark the ch-3 space of the center back shell and move marker up as you go.*

Rnd 1 (WS): Ch 3 (equals dc), 2 dc in first sc, [skip next 4 sc, 3 dc in next sc, ch 3, 3 dc in next sc] 15 (17, 19 , 21, 23) times, end with skip next 4 sc, 3 dc in last sc, dc in 3rd ch of beginning ch (counts as last ch-3 space) to complete center back shell, mark this ch–space, turn. (16 [18, 20, 22, 24] shells).

Rnds 2–6: Work basic pattern rnds Pattern A–D once, then work Pattern A once more (16 [(8, 20, 22, 24] 5–dc blocks).

Next round, increases at four points evenly spaced around.

Rnd 7: Ch 3, 2 dc in beginning space, shell in each of next 1 (1, 2, 2, 2) ch-4 spaces, *(3 dc, ch 3, 3 dc, ch 3, 3 dc) in next ch-4 space for increase, shell in each of next 3 (4, 4, 5, 6) ch-4 spaces, across one side of skirt, (3 dc, ch 3, 3 dc, ch 3, 3 dc) in next ch-4 space for increase, shell in each of next 3 (3, 4, 4, 4) ch-4 spaces across front of skirt, (3 dc, ch 3, 3 dc, ch 3, 3 dc) in next ch-4 space for increase, shell in each of next 3 (4, 4, 5, 6) ch-4 spaces across other side of skirt, (3 dc, ch 3, 3 dc, ch 3, 3 dc) in next ch-4 space for increase, shell in last ch-4 space, end with 3 dc in same space as beginning, ch 2, sc in 3rd ch of beginning ch, turn.

Rnd 8: Ch 3 (counts as dc), 4 dc in beginning space, [ch 4, 5 dc in next ch-3 space] around, end with ch 1, dc in 3rd ch of beginning ch (counts as last ch-4 space), turn. (20 [22, 24, 26, 28] 5-dc blocks)

Rnds 9–25: Work Pattern Rnd D, then rep pattern Rnds A–D (4 times), or for length of skirt desired. Fasten off.

Weave in ends. Block skirt to finished measurements.

Top

Foundation: Work 90 (90, 90, 100, 100) Fsc, Sl st in beg sc to form a ring, being careful not to twist foundation; do not turn, RS of sc edge still facing, begin work across sc of foundation.

Collar

Make a ribbed band across the sc edge of the foundation in the same way as the skirt waistband, only without elastic, one stitch narrower.

Row 1 (RS): Ch 6, do not turn.

Row 2 (RS): Rotate and work in RS face of chains just made, Sl st in 2nd ch from hook, Sl st in each ch across, turn. (5 Sl sts)

Row 3 (WS): With feed yarn now to the back of work as usual, moving backwards (left to right), Sl st in each of next 2 sc of foundation; now moving forwards (right to left) skip 2 Sl sts just made, Sl st in back loop of next 5 Sl sts, turn.

Row 4 (RS): Ch 1, skip ch-1 just made, Sl st in back loop of next 5 Sl sts, turn.

Rows 5–90 (90, 90, 100, 100): Repeat Rows 3–4 across sc of foundation.

Finish collar in same way as waistband finishing, seaming 5 sts.

Yoke

For a better fit, the back neck is raised slightly by creating a short row across 34 (34, 34, 39, 39) sts centered at back neck.

With RS of collar facing, with chain edge of foundation now on top, join yarn with Sl st in chain corresponding to the first row of ribbed band, now the center back of neck.

Skip marked chain, moving to the right, skip back next 16 (16, 16, 19, 19) chs, join yarn with Sl st in next ch.

Short Row (RS): Ch 4, skip next 3 sc, [5 dc in next sc, ch 4, skip next 4 sc] 5 (5, 5, 6, 6) times, 5 dc in next sc, ch 1, skip next 3 sc, dc in next sc (equals ch-4 space), turn. (6 [6, 6, 7, 7] 5-dc blocks)

Next round creates four increase points.

Rnd 1 (WS): Ch 3 (counts as dc), (2 dc, ch 3, 3 dc) in beginning space, shell in each of next 5 (5, 5, 6, 6) ch-4 spaces, (3 dc, ch 3, 3 dc, ch 3, 3 dc) in last ch-4 space of short row for increase; now working across chs of foundation, skip next 2 chs, [3 dc in next ch, ch 3, 3 dc in next ch, skip next 3 chs] twice, shell in next ch, ch 3, 3 dc in next ch for increase, [skip next 3 chs, 3 dc in next ch, ch 3, 3 dc in next ch] 5 (5, 5, 6, 6) times, skip next 3 chs, 3 dc in next ch, ch 3, shell in next ch for increase, [skip next 3 chs, 3 dc in next ch, ch 3, 3 dc in next ch] twice, skip remaining 2 ch sts, 3 dc in same ch-space as beginning, ch 2, sc in top of beginning ch-3 (equals ch-3 space) to complete beginning increase, turn. (22 [22, 22, 24, 24] ch-3 spaces)

At each increase point is (3 dc, ch 3, 3 dc, ch 3, 3 dc); mark 2nd 3-dc group at center of each increase and move or wrap markers up as work progresses.

Rnd 2 (RS): Ch 3 (counts as dc), 4 dc in beginning space, ch 4, [shell in next ch-3 space, ch 4] around, end with ch 1, dc in top of beginning ch-3 (equals ch-4 space), turn. (22 [22, 22, 24, 24] 5-dc blocks, with markers in corner ch-4 spaces between blocks, dividing the yoke into sections of 7 [7, 7, 8, 8] blocks at back and at front, 4 blocks all sizes at each shoulder)

Rnd 3 (WS): Ch 3, (2 dc, ch 3, 3 dc) in beginning space, shell in each ch-4 space across to next marked corner ch-4 space, (3 dc, ch 3, 3 dc, ch 3, 3 dc) for increase in marked ch-4 sp; rep from * twice, shell in each ch-4 space around, ending with 3 dc in same space as beginning, ch 2, sc in 3rd ch of beginning ch, turn. (26 [26, 26, 28, 28] ch-3 sps)

Rnd 4: Work Pattern Rnd C. (26 [26, 26, 28, 28] 5-dc blocks)

Size S only

Rnds 5–6: Repeat Rnds 2–3 once. (30 5-dc blocks)

Sizes M and L Only

Rnds 5–8: Repeat Rnds 2–3 twice. (34 [36] 5-dc blocks)

Size XL Only

Rnds 5–10: Repeat Rnds 2–3 for 3 times. (40 5-dc blocks)

All Sizes

Rnds 5 (7, 9, 9, 11)–8 (10, 12, 12, 14): Work pattern Rnd D once, then work pattern Rnds A–C once. (26 [30, 34, 36, 40] 5-dc blocks)

Body

Note: The markers should be in the four corner ch-4 spaces, dividing the yoke into sections; 8 (9, 10, 11,12) 5–dc blocks in back section and in front section, 5 (6, 7, 7, 8) 5-dc blocks in each armhole section. Next round, connect back and front sections from corner to corner, skipping armhole sections, forming a continuous body round. Folding the yoke in half at the shoulders will help you with the connections. Begin by working from one corner across the back section.

Connect Body Rnd (WS): Ch 3, 2 dc in marked beginning corner space, shell in each of next 7 (8, 9, 10, 11) ch-4 spaces across back section, shell in next marked corner ch-4 space, skip next 5 (6, 7, 7, 8) 5–dc blocks for armhole, shell in next marked corner ch-4 space, shell in each of next 7 (8, 9, 10, 11) ch-4 spaces across front section, shell in next marked corner ch-4 space, skip next 5 (6, 7, 7, 8) 5-dc blocks for other armhole, ending with 3 dc in same corner space as beginning, dc in 3rd ch of beginning ch, turn. (18 [20, 22, 24, 26] shells)

The rounds are now joined at the right–hand underarm. Leave the markers in place at the 4 ch-4 space corners for sleeves later. Next round creates four decreases for body taper; begin by working across body front.

Rnd 1 (RS): Ch 7, [5 dc in ch-3 space of next shell, ch 4] twice, *[3 dc in ch-3 space of next shell, ch 4] twice, [5 dc in ch-3 space of next shell, ch 4] 1 (2, 3, 4, 5) times, [3 dc in ch-3 space of next shell, ch 4] twice*, [5 dc in ch-3 space of next shell, ch 4] 4 times across left–hand underarm; rep from * to * once, 5 dc in ch-3 space of next shell, ch 4, ending with 4 dc in same space as beginning, Sl st in 3rd ch of beginning ch, Sl st in each of next 2 chs of beginning space, turn. (18 [20, 22, 24, 26] ch-4 spaces)

Rnd 2 (WS): Ch 3, 2 dc in beginning space, shell in each of next 2 ch-4 spaces to next 3–dc block, *3 dc in ch-4 space between 3–dc blocks, shell in each of next 2 (3, 4, 5, 6) ch-4 spaces to next 3-dc block, 3 dc in ch-4 space between 3-dc blocks*, shell in each of next 5 ch-4 spaces to next 3-dc block; rep from * to * once, shell in each of next 2 ch-4 spaces, ending with 3 dc in same space as beginning, ch 2, sc in 3rd ch of beginning ch, turn. (14 [16, 18, 20, 22] ch-3 spaces.

Rnd 3: Work Pattern Rnd C, skipping the 3 dc at each decrease point. (14 [16, 18, 20, 22] 5-dc blocks)

Rnds 4–6: Work Pattern Rnd D once, then work Pattern Rnds A–B once. Fasten off.

Tip: To lengthen the body, continue with pattern Rnds C–D, then rep pattern rnds as desired; ending by working either pattern Rnd B or D (shells). Fasten off.

Sleeves

With WS of one underarm facing, skip the two dc row edges of the shells that meet at the center of the underarm (these shells connect the marked corner ch-4 spaces during the connect body round). Join yarn with Sl st in the marked partial corner ch-4 space just past the underarm connection (this corner space was previously worked during connect body round).

Rnd 1 (WS): Ch 3, 2 dc in same space, shell in each of next 4 (5, 6, 6, 7) ch-4 spaces around armhole, 3 dc in the partial corner ch-4 space just before the underarm join, ch 3, 3 dc in each of next 2 dc row edges of join, end with dc in 3rd ch of beginning ch (equals ch-3 space), turn. (6 [7, 8, 8, 9] shells)

Rnds 2–4: Work Pattern Rnds A–C.

Rnd 5: Work Pattern Rnd B.

Begin sleeve taper, decrease by placing 3-dc blocks on either side of center of underarm.

Rnd 6: Ch 3, 2 dc in beginning space, ch 4, 3 dc in ch-3 space of next shell, [ch 4, 5 dc in ch-3 space of next shell] 4 (5, 6, 6, 7) times, ending with ch 1, dc in 3rd ch of beginning ch, turn.

Rnd 7: Ch 3, 2 dc in beginning space, shell in each of next 4 (5, 6, 6, 7) ch-4 spaces, 3 dc in ch-4 space between 3-dc blocks, ending with 3 dc in same space as beginning, dc in 3rd ch of beginning ch, turn.

Rnd 8: Work Pattern Rnd A, skipping 3-dc block of decrease. (5 [6, 7, 7, 8] 5–dc blocks)

Rnd 9: Work Pattern Rnd B. (5 [6, 7, 7, 8] shells)

Create a round of solid dc, adjusting count to be an even number.

Rnd 10 (RS): Ch 3, work 5 (4, 5, 5, 4) dc in beginning space, [dc in next dc, skip next 4 dc, dc in next dc, 5 dc in next ch-3 space] 4 (5, 6, 6, 7) times, dc in next dc, skip next 4 dc, dc in next dc, end with Sl st in top of beginning ch-3, do not turn. (36 [42, 50, 50, 56] dc)

Sleeve Band

Continue to make a ribbed band across dc of sleeve edge, similar to collar.

Row 1 (RS): Ch 6, do not turn.

Row 2 (RS): Rotate and work in RS face of chains just made, Sl st in 2nd ch from hook, Sl st in each ch across, turn. (5 Sl sts)

Row 3 (WS): With feed yarn now to the back of work as usual, moving backwards (left to right), Sl st in each of next 2 sc of foundation; now moving forwards (right to left) skip 2 Sl sts just made, Sl st in back loop of next 5 Sl sts, turn.

Row 4 (RS): Ch 1, skip ch-1 just made, Sl
st in back loop of next 5 Sl sts, turn.

Rows 5–36 (42, 50, 50, 56): Repeat
Rows 3–4 across dc of sleeve edge.

Finish sleeve band in same way as waistband finishing, seaming 5 sts.

Make sleeve and band around other
armhole in the same way.

Weave in ends. Block top to finished
measurements.

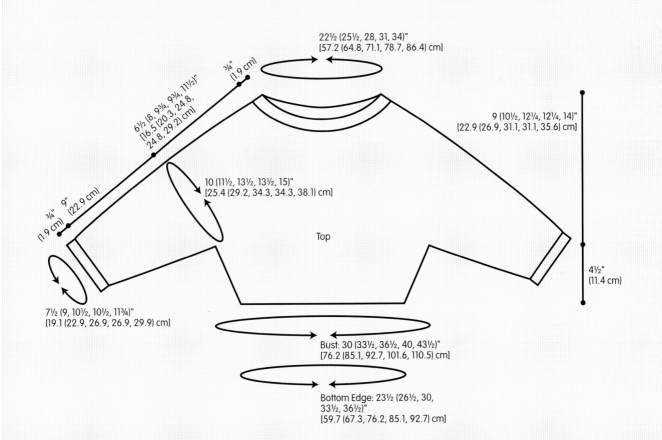

22½ (25½, 28, 31, 34)"
[57.2 (64.8, 71.1, 78.7, 86.4) cm]

¾"
(1.9 cm)

6½ (8, 9¾, 9¾, 11½)"
[16.5 (20.3, 24.8,
24.8, 29.2) cm]

9 (10½, 12¼, 12¼, 14)"
[22.9 (26.9, 31.1, 31.1, 35.6) cm]

10 (11½, 13½, 13½, 15)"
[25.4 (29.2, 34.3, 34.3, 38.1) cm]

¾"   9"
(1.9 cm) (22.9 cm)

Top

4½"
(11.4 cm)

7½ (9, 10½, 10½, 11¾)"
[19.1 (22.9, 26.9, 26.9, 29.9) cm]

Bust: 30 (33½, 36½, 40, 43½)"
[76.2 (85.1, 92.7, 101.6, 110.5) cm]

Bottom Edge: 23½ (26½, 30,
33½, 36½)"
[59.7 (67.3, 76.2, 85.1, 92.7) cm]

Skill Level

Experienced

Yarn

Malabrigo Sock yarn, 100%
Superwash Merino Wool, 440
yd (402 m), 3.5 oz (100g): 5 (5, 6)
hanks #809 Solis

off the shoulder dress

Another piece that was inspired
by recent runway shows is the Off
the Shoulder Dress. It is a classic
style that looks incredible on almost
every woman whether worn close
to the body or with more ease and
movement. This version is stitched
in Malabrigo Sock Weight Yarn,
which keeps the dress light and easy
to wear in all seasons. The Off the
Shoulder Dress can be worn alone for
a night out on the town, or with slacks
or jeans for a more casual look. Either
way you will look as good as you
feel wearing it. If you decide to wear
the folded neck over your shoulders
simply pull it up and drape it like an
oversized cowl.

Designed by
Shannon
Mullett-Bowlsby

Hook

2/C (2.75 mm)

Gauge

Blocked: 40 sts = 6 ¼" (16 cm); 11 rows = 4" (10 cm) in main body pattern

Relaxed: 27 sts and 32 rows = 4" (10 cm) in ribbing pattern

Stretched: 27 sts = 3 ¾" (9.5 cm); 22 rows = 4" (10 cm) in ribbing pattern

Notions

Yarn needle

Finished Sizes

Women's sizes S (M, L)

To fit bust size: 32 (36, 40)" (81.5 [91.5, 101.5] cm)

Finished bust: 34 (38, 42)" (86.5 [96.5, 106.5] cm)

Finished waist: 26 (30, 34)" (66 [76, 86.5] cm)

Finished length: 29 (29 ¾, 30 ¾)" (73.5 [75.5, 78] cm), excluding collar

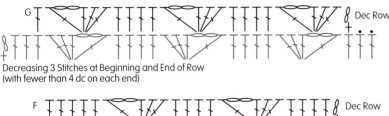

Decreasing 3 Stitches at Beginning and End of Row (with fewer than 4 dc on each end)

Decreasing 3 Stitches at Beginning and End of Row (with more than 4dc on each end)

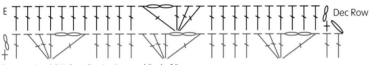

Decreasing 1 Stitch at Beginning and End of Row (with 2 dc on each end)

Decreasing 1 Stitch at Beginning and End of Row (with more than 2 dc on each end)

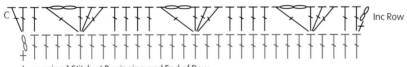

Increasing 1 Stitch at Beginning and End of Row (with more than 11 dc on each end)

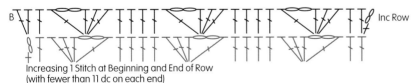

Increasing 1 Stitch at Beginning and End of Row (with fewer than 11 dc on each end)

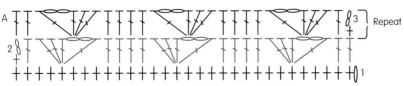

Reduced Sample of Main Body Pattern

Special Stitches

First-dc (first double crochet): *Sc in first st, ch 2. DO NOT ch 1 at the beginning of the row before the sc. Use this stitch, whenever the first stitch of a row is a dc.*

Foundation single crochet (fsc): *Start with a slip knot, ch 2, insert hook in 2nd ch from hook, draw up a loop, yo, draw through 1 loop, yo, and draw through 2 loops – 1 single crochet with its own chain at bottom. Work next stitch under loops of that chain. Insert hook under 2 loops at bottom of the previous stitch, draw up a loop, yo and draw through 1 loop, yo and draw through 2 loops. Repeat for length of foundation.*

Shell: *(3 dc, ch 2, dc) in indicated st or space.*

Pattern Stitches

Ribbing

Row 1: *Ch 1, sc in first st, sc in back loop only of each st across to last st, sc in last st, turn.*

Repeat Row 1 for ribbing pattern.

Main Body Pattern (multiple of 10 sts)

Row 1: *First-dc, dc in next st, sk next 2 sts, shell in next st, *sk next 3 sts, dc in next 4 sts, sk next 2 sts, shell in next st; repeat from * across to last 5 sts, sk next 3 sts, dc in last 2 sts, turn.*

Row 2: *First dc, dc in next st, shell in next ch-2 sp, *sk next 3 dc (the 3 dc of the shell just worked into), dc in next 4 sts, shell in next ch-2 sp; repeat from * across to last 5 sts, sk next 3 dc, dc in last 2 sts, turn.*

Repeat Row 2 for main body pattern.

To work even in main body pattern "as established"

Dc in each dc across to first shell, *shell in next ch-2 sp, sk next 3 dc, dc in next 4 sts; repeat from * across to last shell, shell in next ch-2 sp, dc in each dc to end of row, turn.

To increase 1 stitch at beginning and end of a row in main body pattern

1. If there are fewer than 11 dc before the first shell, increase as follows: (First-dc, dc) in first st, dc in each st across to first shell, *shell in next ch-2 sp, sk next 3 dc, dc in next 4 sts; repeat from * across to last shell, shell in next ch-2 sp, dc in each st across to last st, 2 dc in last st, turn.

2. If there are 11 dc before the first shell, increase as follows: (First-dc, dc) in first st, sk next 2 sts, shell in next st, sk next 3 sts, dc in next 4 sts, *shell in next ch-2 sp, sk next 3 dc, dc in next 4 sts; repeat from * across to last 7 sts, sk next 2 sts, shell in next st, sk next 3 sts, 2 dc in last st, turn.

To increase 1 stitch at beginning of a row in main body pattern

1. If there are fewer than 11 dc before the first shell, increase as follows: (First-dc, dc) in first st, dc in each st across to first shell, *shell in next ch-2 sp, sk next 3 dc, dc in next 4 sts; repeat from * across to last shell, shell in next ch-2 sp, dc in each st to end of row, turn.

2. If there are 11 dc before the first shell, increase as follows: (First-dc, dc) in first st, sk next 2 sts, shell in next st, sk next 3 sts, dc in next 4 sts, *shell in next ch-2 sp, sk next 3 dc, dc in next 4 sts; repeat from * across to last shell, shell in next ch-2 sp, sk next 3 dc, dc in each st to end of row, turn.

To decrease 1 stitch at beginning and end of a row in main body pattern

1. If there are more than 2 dc before the first shell, decrease as follows: Ch 1, sk first st, First-dc in next st, dc in each st to first shell, *shell in next ch-2 sp, sk next 3 dc, dc in next 4 sts; across to last shell, shell in next ch-2 sp, sk next 3 dc, dc in each st to last st, turn; leave last st unworked.

2. If there are 2 dc before the first shell, decrease as follows: Ch 1, sk first st, First-dc in next st, dc in next st, dc in next 2 ch, dc in next 7 dc, *shell in next ch-2 sp, sk next 3 dc, dc in next 4 sts; repeat from * across to last shell, dc in first dc of shell, dc in next 2 ch, dc in next 3 dc, dc in next st, turn; leave last st unworked.

To decrease 3 stitches at beginning and end of a row in main body pattern

1. If there are more than 4 dc before the first shell, decrease as follows: Ch 1, sk first st, Sl st in next 2 sts, First-dc in next st, dc in each st to first shell, *shell in next ch-2 sp, sk next 3 dc, dc in next 4 sts; across to last shell, shell in next ch-2 sp, sk next 3 dc, dc in each st to last 3 sts, turn; leave last 3 sts unworked.

2. If there are 4 dc or fewer before the first shell, decrease as follows: Ch 1, sk first st, Sl st in next 2 sts, First-dc in next st, dc in each remaining ch and st of the first shell, dc in next 4 dc, *shell in next ch-2 sp, sk next 3 dc, dc in next 4 sts; repeat from * across to last shell, dc in each ch and st of the last shell to last 3 sts, turn; leave last 3 sts unworked.

Body Panel
(Make 2)

Ribbed Hem
Row 1: Work 19 (21, 23) Fsc, turn.
Work in ribbing pattern for a total of 116 (130, 144) rows. Piece should measure about 17 (19, 21)" (43 [48.5, 53.5] cm) from beginning, slightly stretched.

Main Body
Row 1: Ch 1, working in ends of rows across long edge of ribbing, [sc in end of next 14 (9, 6) rows, sc2tog] 6 (10, 14) times, sc in end of each remaining row across, turn. (110 [120, 130] sts)
Work in main body pattern until piece measures about 25 (25¼, 25½)" (63.5 [64, 65] cm) from beginning.

Shape Raglan Armholes
Row 1: Sl st in first 3 dc, Sl st in next 2 ch, (First-dc, dc) in next dc, sk next 2 sts, dc in next 4 sts, *shell in next ch-2 sp, sk next 3 dc, dc in next 4 sts; repeat from * across to last shell, sk next dc, sk next ch, 2 dc in next ch; leave remaining sts unworked. (98 [108, 118] sts).

Note: *See instructions for decreasing 1 stitch at the beginning and end of a row in Pattern Stitches section.*

Rows 2–11 (12, 14): Work in main body pattern as established, AND decrease 1 stitch at beginning and end of each row. (78 [86, 92] sts remain)
Fasten off. Armhole should measure about 4 (4½, 5)" (10 [11.5, 12.5] cm), measured straight up.

Sleeve

(Make 2)

Ribbed Cuff

Row 1: Fsc 14 sts, turn.

Work in ribbing pattern for a total of 41 (45, 48) rows. Piece should measure about 6 (6½, 7)" (15 [16.5, 18] cm) from beginning, slightly stretched.

Main Sleeve

Row 1: Ch 1, working in ends of rows across long edge of ribbing, [sc in end of next 9 (10, 8) rows, sc2tog] 3 (3, 4) times, sc in end of each remaining row across, turn. (38 [42, 44] sts)

Row 2: First-dc, dc in next 5 (2, 3) sts, sk next 2 sts, shell in next st, *sk next 3 sts, dc in next 4 sts, sk next 2 sts, shell in next st; repeat from * across to last 9 (6, 7) sts, sk next 3 sts, dc in last 6 (3, 4) sts, turn. (3 [4, 4] shells)

Next 8 (12, 15) Rows: Work in main body pattern as established AND increase 1 stitch at the beginning and end of each row. (54 [66, 74] sts)

Next 28 (24, 22) Rows: Work in main body pattern as established AND increase 1 stitch at beginning of each row. (82 [90, 96] sts)

Next 3 (3, 4) Rows: Work even in main body pattern as established.

Piece should measure about 15 (15, 15½)" (38 [38, 39.5] cm) from beginning.

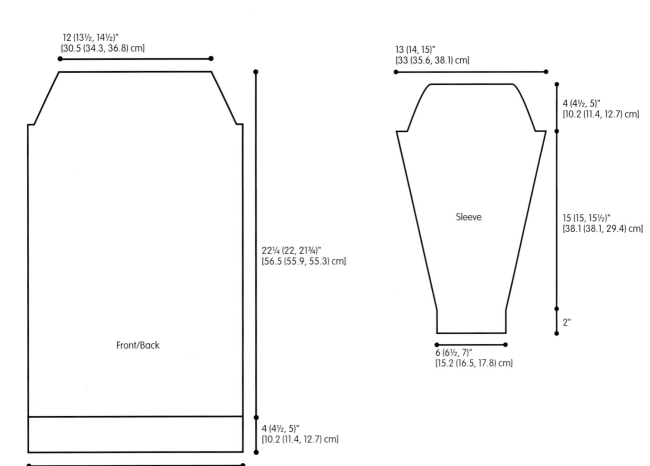

12 (13½, 14½)"
[30.5 (34.3, 36.8) cm]

22¼ (22, 21¾)"
[56.5 (55.9, 55.3) cm]

Front/Back

4 (4½, 5)"
[10.2 (11.4, 12.7) cm]

17 (19, 21)"
[43.2 (48.3, 54.4) cm]

13 (14, 15)"
[33 (35.6, 38.1) cm]

4 (4½, 5)"
[10.2 (11.4, 12.7) cm]

Sleeve

15 (15, 15½)"
[38.1 (38.1, 29.4) cm]

2"

6 (6½, 7)"
[15.2 (16.5, 17.8) cm]

Shape Raglans

Notes: *When working Row 1, count each dc as a st and each ch as a st. When working the end of the row, take care to make it match the beginning of the row. This may require working dc sts into some of the sts of the last shell.*

Row 1: Sl st in first 6 sts, First-dc in next st, dc in each st across to next shell, *shell in next ch-2 sp, sk next 3 dc, dc in next 4 sts; repeat from * across to last 6 sts; leave last 6 sts unworked. (70 [78, 84] sts)

Next 8 (7, 13) Rows: Work in main body pattern as established AND decrease 1 stitch at beginning and end of each row. (54 [64, 58] sts)

Sizes S (M) Only

Next Row: Work even in main body pattern as established.

Next Row: Work in main body pattern as established AND decrease 3 stitches at the beginning and end of row. (48 [58] sts)

Repeat last 2 rows 0 (1) time(s). (48 [52] sts)

All Sizes

Fasten off. Raglans should measure about 4 (4½, 5)" (10 [11.5, 12.5] cm), measured straight up.

Finishing

Block all pieces to finished dimensions. Sew raglan edges of sleeves to raglan armholes of body panels. Sew side and sleeve seams.

Collar

Notes: *Collar is worked in main body pattern over joined and turned rounds. Work first stitch of each round into the same stitch as the Sl st join. Work decreases in each section (body panels, and sleeves) as instructed, in same manner as decreases worked at beginning and end of rows before the pieces were seamed. There should be a total of 252 (276, 300) sts around top edge of seamed piece.*

Join yarn in back raglan seam to work across top back edge.

Round 1 (decrease): Begin working across first body panel. Decrease 1 st at beginning and end of each body panel, decrease 3 sts at beginning and end of each sleeve panel, and work over remainder of main body pattern sts, as follows: *shell in next ch-2 sp, sk next 3 dc, dc in next st, dc2tog, dc in next st; repeat from * around; join with Sl st in first dc, turn.

Round 2 (decrease): Begin working across first sleeve. Decrease 1 st at beginning and end of each body panel, decrease 3 sts at beginning and end of each sleeve panel, and work over remainder of main body pattern sts, as follows: *shell in next ch-2 sp, sk next 3 dc, dc2tog, dc in next st; repeat from * around; join with Sl st in first dc, turn.

Round 3 (decrease): Decrease 1 st at beginning and end of each body panel, decrease 3 sts at beginning and end of each sleeve panel, and work over remainder of main body pattern sts, as follows: *shell in next ch-2 sp, sk next 3 dc, dc2tog; repeat from * around; join with Sl st in first dc, turn.

Round 4 (decrease): Decrease 1 st at beginning and end of each body panel, decrease 3 sts at beginning and end of each sleeve panel, and work over remainder of main body pattern sts, as follows: *shell in next ch-2 sp, sk next 3 dc, dc in next st**; repeat from * around; join with Sl st in first dc, turn.

Rounds 5 and 6: Work even in established pattern with no decreases.

Begin Increases

Round 7: Dc in each dc at beginning and end of each body panel and sleeve to first shell, and work over remainder of main body pattern sts, as follows: *shell in next ch-2 sp, sk next 3 dc, 2 dc in next st; repeat from * around; join with Sl st in first dc, turn.

Round 8: Dc in each dc at beginning and end of each body panel and sleeve to first shell, and work over remainder of main body pattern sts, as follows: *shell in next ch-2 sp, sk next 3 dc, dc in next st, 2 dc in next st; repeat from * around; join with Sl st in first dc, turn.

Round 9: Dc in each dc at beginning and end of each body panel and sleeve to first shell, and work over remainder of main body pattern sts, as follows: *shell in next ch-2 sp, sk next 3 dc, dc in next st, 2 dc in next st, dc in next st; repeat from * around; join with Sl st in first dc, turn.

Rounds 10–25: Work even in established pattern.

Fasten off. Weave in ends.

Skill Level

Intermediate

Yarn

Handmaiden yarn, Sea Silk, (70% Silk, 30% Seacell; 3.5oz/100g; 437yds/400m): Color Cezanne 4 (4, 5) balls

cross front halter dress

In fashion, what was old is new again. Many current designers are pulling inspiration from past trends, like I am doing with the Cross Front Halter Dress. There are few dresses more elegant and feminine than the halter dress. They are as classy as they are classic. My version, stitched in Hand Maiden Sea Silk, includes an open lace pattern skirt, a structured midriff, and more lace to be draped around the neck. The addition of the zipper up the back aids in dressing. Wearing a slip under the Halter Dress will give you a sleek, chic look for evening or even a casual day out. Worn over a bathing suit the Halter Dress is an upgrade to the usual beach cover-up.

Designed by
Shannon
Mullett-Bowlsby

Hook	Gauge	Notions	Finished Sizes
3/D (3.25 mm)	Skirt (blocked)	Yarn needle	Women's sizes S (M, L)
2/C (2.75 mm)	51 sts = 9" (23 cm); 12 rows = 6" (15 cm) in Skirt 1 pattern with 2/C (2.75 mm) hook.	Zipper (optional), 6–8" (15-20.5 cm) long	To fit bust size: 32 (36, 40)" (81.5 [91.5, 101.5] cm)
1/B (2.25 mm)	51 sts = 11½" (29 cm); 7 rows = 5" (12.5 cm) in Skirt 2 pattern with 3/D (3.25 mm) hook.		Finished bust: 34 (38, 42)" (86.5 [96.5, 106.5] cm)
	Midriff (blocked)		Finished waist: 30 (32, 34)" (76 [81.5, 86.5] cm)
	38 sts = 5½" (14 cm); 28 rows = 4" (10 cm) in Midriff pattern with 1/B (2.25 mm) hook.		Finished hip: 36 (42, 44)" (91.5 [106.5, 112] cm)
	Halter top (blocked)		
Reduced Sample of Skirt Pattern	51 sts = 11" (28 cm); 8 rows = 4" (10 cm) in Skirt 2 pattern with 2/C (2.75 mm) hook.		

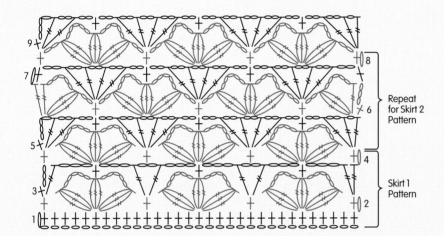

Notes

1. Dress is made from the center out, beginning at waist.

2. Skirt is worked from waist down.

3. Stitches are picked up across the waist edge of skirt and midriff is worked upward.

4. Halter section is worked separately and sewn to top of midriff.

Special Stitches

Cluster (Cl): [yarn over] twice, insert hook in indicated stitch, yarn over and draw up a loop, [yarn over and draw through 2 loops on hook] twice (2 loops remain on hook), *[yarn over] twice, insert hook in same stitch, yarn over and draw up a loop, [yarn over and draw through 2 loops on hook] twice; repeat from * once more, yarn over and draw through all 4 loops on hook.

Cluster Fan (Cl-Fan): ([Cl, ch 5] twice, Cl) in indicated stitch or space.

Fan: ([Tr, ch 2] 3 times, tr) in indicated stitch.

First treble crochet (First-tr): Sc in first st, ch 3. Notes: Do NOT ch 1 at the beginning of the row before sc. Use this stitch, whenever the first stitch of a row is a tr.

Foundation single crochet (fsc): Start with a slip knot, ch 2, insert hook in 2nd ch from hook, draw up a loop, yo, draw through 1 loop, yo, and draw through 2 loops—1 single crochet with its own chain at bottom. Work next stitch under loops of that chain. Insert hook under 2 loops at bottom of the previous stitch, draw up a loop, yo and draw through 1 loop, yo and draw through 2 loops. Repeat for length of foundation.

Single crochet 2 together (sc2tog): [Insert hook in next stitch, yarn over and draw up a loop] twice, yarn over and draw through all 3 loops on hook.

V-st (V-stitch): (Tr, ch 2, tr) in indicated stitch.

Skirt

Skirt 1 Pattern

Row 1: With C-2 (2.75mm) hook, work 171 (181, 191) Fsc, turn.

Row 2: Ch 1, sc in first st, *skip next 4 sts, Cl-Fan in next st, skip next 4 sts, sc in next st; repeat from * across, turn. (17 [18, 19] Cl-Fans)

Row 3: (First-tr, tr) in first st, ch 3, sc in center Cl of next Cl-Fan, *ch 3, V-st in next sc, ch 3, sc in center Cl of next Cl-Fan; repeat from * across to last sc, ch 3, 2 tr in last sc, turn. (16 [17, 18] V-sts)

Row 4: Ch 1, sc in first st, skip next ch-3 sp, Cl-Fan in next sc, *skip next ch-3 sp, sc in next ch-2 sp, skip next ch-3 sp, Cl-Fan in next sc; repeat from * across to last 2 tr, skip next tr, sc in last tr, turn.

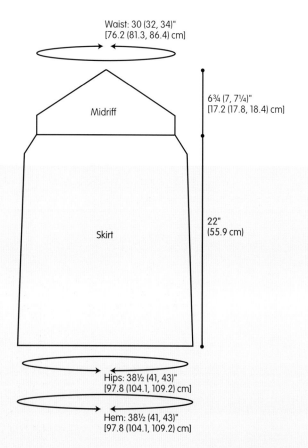

Waist: 30 (32, 34)"
[76.2 (81.3, 86.4) cm]

Midriff

6¾ (7, 7¼)"
[17.2 (17.8, 18.4) cm]

Skirt

22"
(55.9 cm)

Hips: 38½ (41, 43)"
[97.8 (104.1, 109.2) cm]

Hem: 38½ (41, 43)"
[97.8 (104.1, 109.2) cm]

Skirt 2 Pattern

Change to D-3 (3.25mm) hook.

Row 5: (First-tr, ch 1, tr, ch 2, tr) in first st, ch 2, sc in center Cl of next Cl-Fan, *ch 2, Fan in next sc, ch 2, sc in center Cl of next Cl-Fan; repeat from * across to last sc, ch 2, (tr, ch 2, tr, ch 1, tr) in last sc, turn.

Row 6: First-tr, (tr, ch 5, Cl) in next ch-1 sp, ch 2, skip next 2 ch-sps, sc in next sc, *ch 2, skip next 2 ch-sps, Cl-Fan in next ch-2 sp, ch 2, skip next 2 ch-sps, sc in next sc; repeat from * across to last 3 ch-sps, ch 2, skip next 2 ch-sps, (Cl, ch 5, tr) in last ch-1 sp, tr in last tr, turn.

Row 7: Ch 1, sc in first st, ch 2, skip first 2 ch-sps, Fan in next sc, *ch 2, skip next 2 ch-sps, sc in center Cl of next Cl-Fan, ch 2, skip next 2 ch-sps, Fan in next sc; repeat from * across to last 2 ch-sps, ch 2, skip last 2 ch-sps, sc in last tr, turn.

Row 8: Ch 1, sc in first st, *ch 2, skip next 2 ch-sps, Cl-Fan in next ch-sp (center ch-sps of Fan), ch 2, skip next 2 ch-sps, sc in next sc; repeat from * across, turn.

Repeat last 4 rows until skirt measures about 22" (56 cm) from beginning. Fasten off.

Midriff

Row 1 (increase): With 1/B (2.25 mm) hook, working across "chain" side of skirt foundation, join yarn with sc in first st, sc in next 6 (2, 0) sts, 2 sc in next st, [sc in next 3 sts, 2 sc in next st] twice, [sc in next 3 sts, 2 sc in next st, sc in next 4 sts, 2 sc in next st] 15 (17, 19) times, [sc in next 3 sts, 2 sc in next st] 3 (3, 2) times, sc in next 8 (4, 1) sts, 2 sc in last 0 (0, 1) st, turn. (207 [221, 235] sts)

Rows 2–14: Ch 1, sc in first st, sc FL in each st across to last st, sc in last st, turn. Fasten off. Midriff should measures about 2" (5 cm).

Row 15: Skip first 52 (55, 58) sts of last row, join yarn with sc in next st, [sc2tog] twice, sc in front loop only of next 95 (103, 111) sts, sc2tog in front loop only of next 2 sts, sc in next st, turn; leave remaining sts unworked. (100 [108, 116] sts)

Rows 16–43: Ch 1, [sc2tog] twice, sc in front loop only of each st across to last 3 sts, sc2tog sc in front loop only of, sc in last st, turn. (16 [24, 32] sts)

Rows 44–45 (47, 49): Ch 1, sc in first st, [sc2tog] twice, sc sc in front loop only of each st across to last 3 sts, [sc2tog] twice, sc in last st, turn. (8 sts)

Next Row: Ch 1, [sc2tog] 4 times, turn. (4 sts)

Next Row: Ch 1, [sc2tog] twice, turn. (2 sts)

Next Row: Ch 1, [sc2tog. (1 st)

Midriff should measure about 6 ¾ (7, 7 ¼)" (17 [18, 18.5] cm) from beginning. Fasten off.

Halter Top Section

(Make 2)

Row 1: With 2/C (2.75 mm) hook, work 41 Fsc, turn.

Row 2: (First-tr, ch 1, tr, ch 2, tr) in first st (half-Fan made), ch 2, skip next 4 sts, sc in next st, *ch 2, skip next 4 sts, Fan in next sc, ch 2, skip next 4 sts, sc in next st; repeat from * across to last 5 sts, ch 2, skip next 4 sts, (tr, ch 2, tr, ch 1, tr) in last st (half-Fan made), turn. (3 Fans, and 2 half-Fans)

Row 3: First-tr, (tr, ch 5, Cl) in next ch-1 sp, ch 2, skip next 2 ch-sps, sc in next sc, *ch 2, skip next 2 ch-sps, Cl-Fan in next ch-2 sp, ch 2, skip next 2 ch-sps, sc in next sc; repeat from * across to last 3 ch-sps, ch 2, skip next 2 ch-sps, (Cl, ch 5, tr) in last ch-1 sp, tr in last tr, turn.

Row 4: Ch 1, sc in first st, ch 2, skip next 2 ch-sps, Fan in next sc, *ch 2, skip next 2 ch-sps, sc in center Cl of next Cl-Fan, ch 2, skip next 2 ch-sps, Fan in next sc; repeat from * across to last 2 ch-sps, ch 2, skip last 2 ch-sps, sc in last tr, turn.

Row 5: Ch 1, sc in first st, *ch 2, skip next 2 ch-sps, Cl-Fan in next ch-sp, ch 2, skip next 2 ch-sps, sc in next sc; repeat from * across, turn.

Repeat last 4 rows until piece measures about 48 (50, 52)" (122 [127, 132] cm) from beginning. Fasten off.

```
┌──────────────────────────────────────────────┐  ┊
│                                                │  9"
│                  Halter Top                    │  (22.9 cm)
│                                                │  ┊
└──────────────────────────────────────────────┘
```
48 (50, 52)"
[122 (127, 132) cm]

Finishing

Attach Halter Top Sections to Midriff

Lay skirt/midriff piece flat. Place one halter top section across top edge of midriff, with one short end of halter top section in line with straight side edge of skirt/midriff and long side edge of halter top section place against curved edge of midriff to point. Sew long side edge of halter top section to curved top edge of midriff, sewing only from beginning of halter top section to center point of midriff, leaving remainder of halter top section unsewn for tying behind neck. repeat to sew 2nd halter top section to skirt/midriff.

Sew seam up back of skirt to desired height for applying optional zipper.

Sew zipper into back of garment.

Weave in any remaining ends.

Skill Level

Intermediate

Yarn

Lucci yarn Cotton Tape (www.
lucciyarn.com) #20075, 100%
mercerized cotton, 1900 yd (1737
m), 16 oz (453 g) per cone OR
210 yd (240 m), 1.75 oz (50 g) per
skein (CYCA category 2 Fine): 6 (7,
7, 8) skeins OR one pound cone
in Rust

cosmopolitan cocktail skirt

With inspiration drawn from vintage
thread crochet doilies, this skirt turns
what could be considered fussy
and demure into a bold fashion
statement. Traditional doily elements
such as filet mesh, shells and
pineapples are given a fresh twist by
exploding the lace using sport weight
yarn and a relaxed gauge. The skirt
is completely seamless and has a
modified circular shape. It is slim-
fitting through high hip, then flared
to a generous full hip and spectacular
hem that sweeps in soft waves at
lower calf length. The drawstring
waistband has plenty of stretch to pull
on and allows for an adjustable fit.

Designed by
Doris Chan

Hook

6/G (4 mm)

Gauge

16 sts = 4" (10 cm); 5 rows dc of skirt yoke = 2" (5 cm); 4 rows (tr, ch 2) mesh = 3" (7.5 cm)

One lace rep at high hip (skirt Rnd 10) = 3½" (9 cm); one lace rep at full hip (skirt Rnd 15) = 4½" (11.5 cm); one lace rep at hem = 11" (28 cm)

Notions

Stitch marker

Tapestry needle

Finished Sizes

Women's sizes S (M, L, XL)

As finished and blocked:

Finished waist: 27 (30, 33, 36)" (68.5 [76, 84, 91.5] cm) with stretch to pull on

Finished high hips: 31½ (35, 38½, 42)" (80 [89, 98, 106.5] cm)

Finished full hips: 40½ (45, 49½, 54)" (103 [114.5, 125.5, 137] cm)

Finished hem: 99 (110, 121, 132)" (251.5 [279.5, 307.5, 335] cm)

Finished length: 29" (73.5 cm)

Notes

Skirt is crocheted from the waist foundation down in joined rounds, RS always facing (not turned after each round). The place where the rounds are joined will be shifted twice; this avoids awkwardness and helps keep the joins nearly invisible.

Special Stitches

Foundation single crochet (fsc): Start with a slip knot, ch 2, insert hook in 2nd ch from hook, draw up a loop, yo, draw through 1 loop, yo, and draw through 2 loops—1 single crochet with its own chain at bottom. Work next stitch under loops of that chain. Insert hook under 2 loops at bottom of the previous stitch, draw up a loop, yo and draw through 1 loop, yo and draw through 2 loops. Repeat for length of foundation.

Spike Sc: Insert hook under chain space 2 rows below, make sc that encloses both chains below.

Tr3tog cluster (Cl): Yo twice, insert hook in st or space indicated, yo and draw up a loop (4 loops on hook), [yo and draw through 2 loops on hook] twice (2 loops remain on hook), yo twice, insert hook in same st or space, yo and draw up a loop (5 loops on hook), [yo and draw through 2 loops on hook] twice (3 loops remain on hook), yo twice, insert hook in same st or space, yo and draw up a loop (6 loops on hook), [yo and draw through 2 loops on hook] twice (4 loops remain on hook), yo and draw through all 4 loops on hook.

Beginning cluster (Beg-Cl): Ch 3 (equals first leg of cluster), in the beginning space, yo twice, insert hook in st or space indicated, yo and draw up a loop (4 loops on hook), [yo and draw through 2 loops on hook] twice (2 loops remain on hook), yo twice, insert hook in same st or space, yo and draw up a loop (5 loops on hook),

[yo and draw through 2 loops on hook] twice (3 loops remain on hook), yo and draw through all 3 loops on hook.

Shell (shell): (Cl, ch 3, Cl) in same st or space.

Hanging Picot (rests between stitches): Ch 3, sc in 3rd ch from hook.

Attached Picot (stuck to the top of a stitch): Ch 3, insert hook through all 7 front loops at the top of the tr6tog cluster just made (in other words, retrace the path of the loop made in the last step of the cluster), Sl st to close picot.

Tr6tog cluster: In ch-3 space of next shell, yo twice, insert hook, yo and draw up a loop (4 loops on hook), [yo and draw through 2 loops on hook] twice (2 loops remain on hook), yo twice, insert hook in same space, yo and draw up a loop (5 loops on hook), [yo and draw through 2 loops on hook] twice (3 loops remain on hook), yo twice, insert hook in same space, yo and draw up a loop (6 loops on hook), [yo and draw through 2 loops on hook] twice (4 loops remain on hook); in ch-3 space of next shell, yo twice, insert hook, yo and draw up a loop (7 loops on hook), [yo and draw through 2 loops on hook] twice (5 loops remain on hook), yo twice, insert hook in same space, yo and draw up a loop (8 loops on hook), [yo and draw through 2 loops on hook] twice (6 loops remain on hook), yo twice, insert hook in same space, yo and draw up a loop (9 loops on hook), [yo and draw through 2 loops on hook] twice (7 loops remain on hook), yo and draw through all 7 loops on hook.

Skirt

Foundation: Work 108 (120, 132, 144) Fsc to measure 27 (30, 33, 36)", Sl st in beg sc to form a ring, being careful not to twist foundation. Mark the foundation

chain under the beginning sc (it has the beginning yarn tail hanging from it) for waistband later.

Now begin work around sc edge of foundation, creating 9 (10, 11, 12) pattern repeats using 12 sts of foundation each repeat.

Rnd 1: Ch 3 (counts as dc here and throughout), skip first sc, dc in each of next 4 sc, [ch 5, skip next 3 sc, dc in each of next 9 sc] 9 (10, 11, 12) times, omitting last 5 dc, join with Sl st in top of beginning ch-3. (9 (10, 11, 12) ch-5 spaces)

Rnd 2: Ch 3, skip first dc, dc in each of next 4 dc, [ch 6, skip next ch-5 space, dc in each of next 9 dc] 9 (10, 11, 12) times, omitting last 5 dc, join with Sl st in top of beginning ch-3.

Rnd 3: Ch 3, skip first dc, dc in each of next 4 dc, [ch 4, spike sc under next ch-space 2 rows below, ch 4, dc in each of next 9 dc] 9 (10, 11, 12) times, omitting last 5 dc, join with Sl st in top of beginning ch-3.

Rnd 4: Ch 3, skip first dc, dc in each of next 4 dc, [ch 6, skip next (ch-4 space, sc, ch-4 space), dc in each of next 9 dc] 9 (10, 11, 12) times, omitting last 5 dc, join with Sl st in top of beginning ch-3.

Rnd 5: Ch 3, skip first dc, dc in each of next 4 dc, [ch 7, skip next ch-6 space, dc in each of next 9 dc] 9 (10, 11, 12) times, omitting last 5 dc, join with Sl st in top of beginning ch-3.

Rnd 6: Ch 3, skip first dc, dc in each of next 4 dc, [ch 5, spike sc under next ch-space 2 rows below, ch 5, dc in each of next 9 dc] 9 (10, 11, 12) times, omitting last 5 dc, join with Sl st in top of beginning ch-3.

Rnd 7: Ch 3, skip first dc, dc in each of next 4 dc, [ch 7, skip next (ch-5 space, sc, ch-5 space), dc in each of next 9 dc] 9 (10, 11, 12) times, omitting last 5 dc, join with Sl st in top of beginning ch-3.

Rnd 8: Ch 3, skip first dc, [dc in each of next 4 dc, ch 7, skip next ch-7 space, dc in each of next 4 dc, 2 dc in next dc] 9 (10,

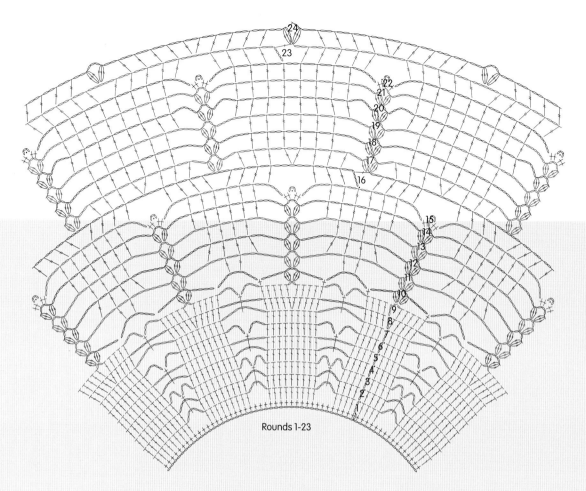

Rounds 1-23

11, 12) times, omitting last 2 dc, end with dc in same st as beginning, Sl st in 3rd ch of beginning ch.

Rnd 9: Ch 3, skip first dc, dc in each of next 4 dc, [ch 5, spike sc under next ch-space 2 rows below, ch 5, dc in each of next 5 dc, ch 2, dc in each of next 5 dc] 9 (10, 11, 12) times, omitting last (ch 2 and 5 dc), end with ch 1, sc top of beginning ch-3 (equals beginning ch-2 space).

Rnd 10: Beg-Cl, [ch 4, skip next 4 dc, sc in next dc, ch 9, skip next (ch 5, sc, ch 5), sc in next dc, ch 4, skip next 4 dc, shell in next ch-2 sp] 9 (10, 11, 12) times, omitting last shell, end with Cl in same space as beginning, ch 1, hdc in next ch following beginning cluster (equals beginning ch-3 space).

Rnd 11: Beg-Cl, [ch 6, skip next ch-4 space, skip first 3 ch of next ch-9 space, tr in next ch, ch 2, skip next ch, tr in next ch, ch 6, skip next ch-4 space, shell in ch-3 space of next shell] 9 (10, 11, 12) times, omitting last shell, end with Cl in same space as beginning, ch 1, hdc in next ch following beginning cluster.

Rnd 12: Beg-Cl, [ch 6, skip first 3 ch of next ch-6 space, tr in next ch, ch 2, skip remaining 2 ch, tr in next tr, ch 2, skip

next ch-2 space, tr in next tr, ch 2, skip first 2 ch of next ch-6 space, tr in next ch, ch 6, shell in ch-3 space of next shell] 9 (10, 11, 12) times, omitting last shell, end with Cl in same space as beginning, ch 1, hdc in next following beginning cluster.

Rnd 13: Beg-Cl, *ch 6, skip next ch-6 space, tr in next tr, [ch 2, skip next ch-2 space, tr in next tr] 3 times, ch 6, skip next ch-6 space, shell in ch-3 space of next shell*; rep from * to * around, omitting last shell, end with Cl in same space as beginning, ch 1, hdc in next ch following beginning cluster.

Rnd 14: Beg-Cl, *ch 6, skip first 3 ch of next ch-6 space, tr in next ch, ch 2, skip remaining 2 ch, tr in next tr, [ch 2, skip next ch-2 space, tr in next tr] 3 times, ch 2, skip first 2 ch of next ch-6 space, tr in next ch, ch 6, shell in ch-3 space of next shell; rep from * around, omitting last shell, end with Cl in same space as beginning, ch 1, hdc in next ch following beginning cluster.

Rnd 15: Ch 1, 2 sc in beginning space, *ch 6, skip next ch-6 space, tr in next tr, [ch 2, skip next ch-2 space, tr in next tr] 5 times, ch 6, skip next ch-6 space, (2 sc, Hanging Picot, 2 sc) in ch-3 space of next shell;

rep from * around, omitting last 2 sc, end with Sl st in beginning sc. Fasten off.

First shift: With new yarn, skip next 3 tr, join with Sl st in next tr.

Rnd 16: Ch 6 (equals tr, ch 2), *[skip next ch-2 space, tr in next tr, ch 2] twice, skip first 2 ch of next ch-6 space, tr in next ch, ch 5, skip first 3 ch of next ch-6 space, tr in next ch, ch 2, skip remaining 2 ch, tr in next tr, [ch 2, skip next ch-2 space, tr in next tr] twice**, ch 5, skip next ch-2 space, tr in next tr, ch 2; rep from * around, ending last rep at **, end with ch 2, dc in 4th ch of beginning ch-5 (equals beginning ch-5 space).

Rnd 17: Beg-Cl in top of dc that closed previous rnd (to equal placement in 3rd ch of beginning ch-5), *ch 2, skip next (tr and ch-2 space), tr in next tr, [ch 2, skip next ch-2 space, tr in next tr] twice, ch 2, skip first 2 ch of next ch-5 space, (tr, ch 2, tr) in next ch, ch 2, skip remaining 2 ch, tr in next tr, [ch 2, skip next ch-2 space, tr in next tr] twice, ch 2, skip next (ch-2 space and tr), skip first 2 ch of next ch-5 space, shell in next ch; rep from * around, omitting last shell, end with Cl in same top of dc as beginning, ch 1, hdc in next ch following beginning cluster.

Rounds 24-38

Rnd 18: Beg-Cl, *ch 6, skip next (ch-2 space, tr and ch-2 space), tr in next tr, [ch 2, skip next ch-2 space, tr in next tr] 5 times, ch 6, shell in ch-3 space of next shell; rep from * around, omitting last shell, end with Cl in same space as beginning, ch 1, hdc in next ch following beginning cluster.

Rnd 19: Beg-Cl, *ch 6, skip next ch-6 space, tr in next tr, [ch 2, skip next ch-2 space, tr in next tr] 5 times, ch 6, skip next ch-6 space, shell in ch-3 space of next shell; rep from * taround, omitting last shell, end with Cl in same space as beginning, ch 1, hdc in next ch following beginning cluster.

Rnd 20: Beg-Cl, *ch 6, skip first 3 ch of next ch-6 space, tr in next ch, ch 2, skip remaining 2 ch of ch-6 space, tr in next tr, [ch 2, skip next ch-2 space, tr in next tr] 5 times, ch 2, skip first 2 ch of next ch-6 space, tr in next ch, ch 6, shell in ch-3 space of next shell; rep from * around, omitting last shell, end with Cl in same space as beginning, ch 1, hdc in next ch following beginning cluster.

Rnd 21: Beg-Cl, *ch 6, skip next ch-6 space, tr in next tr, [ch 2, skip next ch-2 space, tr in next tr] 7 times, ch 6, skip next ch-6 space, shell in ch-3 space of next shell; rep from * around, omitting last shell, end with Cl in same space as beginning, ch 1, hdc in next ch following beginning cluster.

Rnd 22: Ch 1, 2 sc in beginning space, *ch 6, skip next ch-6 space, tr in next tr, [ch 2, skip next ch-2 space, tr in next tr] 7 times, ch 6, skip next ch-6 space, (2 sc, Hanging Picot, 2 sc) in ch-3 space of next shell; rep from * around, omitting last 2 sc, end with Sl st in beginning sc. Fasten off.

Second shift: With new yarn, skip next 4 tr, join yarn with Sl st in next tr.

Rnd 23: Ch 6 (equals tr, ch 2), *[skip next ch-2 space, tr in next tr, ch 2] 3 times, skip first 2 ch of next ch-6 space, tr in next ch, ch 5, skip first 3 ch of next ch-6 space, tr in next ch, ch 2, skip remaining 2 ch, tr in next tr, [ch 2, skip next ch-2 space, tr in next tr] 3 times**, ch 5, skip next ch-2 space, tr in next tr, ch 2; rep from * around, ending last rep at **, end with ch 2, dc in 4th ch of beginning ch (equals beginning ch-5 space).

Rnd 24: Beg-Cl in top of dc that closed previous rnd (to equal placement in 3rd ch of beginning ch-5), *ch 2, skip next (tr and ch-2 space), tr in next tr, [ch 2, skip next ch-2 space, tr in next tr] 3 times, ch 2, skip first 2 ch of next ch-5 space, (tr, ch 2, tr) in next ch, ch 2, skip remaining 2 ch, tr in next tr, [ch 2, skip next ch-2 space, tr in next tr] 3 times, ch 2, skip next (ch-2 space and tr), skip first 2 ch of next ch-5 space, shell in next ch; rep from * around, omitting last shell, end with Cl in same top of dc as beginning, ch 2, sc in next ch following beginning cluster (equals beginning ch-3 space).

Rnd 25: Beg-Cl, ch 4, *skip next (ch-2 space, tr and ch-2 space), tr in next tr, [ch 2, skip next ch-2 space, tr in next tr] 7 times, ch 4, skip next (ch-2 space, tr and ch-2 space)**, (shell, ch 5, shell) in ch-3 space of next shell; rep from * around, ending last rep at **, end with (shell, ch 5, Cl) in same space as beginning, ch 1, hdc in next ch following beginning cluster.

Rnd 26: Beg-Cl, *ch 4, skip next (ch-4 space, tr and ch-2 space), tr in next tr, [ch 2, skip next ch-2 space, tr in next tr] 5 times, ch 4, skip next (ch-2 space, tr and ch-4 space), shell in ch-3 space of next shell, ch 5, skip first 2 ch of next ch-5 space, (tr, ch 5, tr) in next ch, ch 5, shell in ch-3 space of next shell; rep from * around, omitting last shell, end with Cl in same space as beginning, ch 1, hdc in next ch following beginning cluster.

Rnd 27: Beg-Cl, *ch 4, skip next (ch-4 space, tr and ch-2 space), tr in next tr, [ch 2, skip next ch-2 space, tr in next tr] 3 times, ch 4, skip next (ch-2 space, tr and ch-4 space), shell in ch-3 space of next shell, ch 5, skip next ch-5 space, 9 tr in next ch-5 space, ch 5, skip next ch-5 space, shell in ch-3 space of next shell; rep from * around, omitting last shell, end with Cl in same space as beginning, ch 1, hdc in next ch following beginning cluster.

Rnd 28: Beg-Cl, *ch 4, skip next (ch-4 space, tr and ch-2 space), tr in next tr, ch 2, skip next ch-2 space, tr in next tr, ch 4, skip next (ch-2 space, tr and ch-4 space), shell in ch-3 space of next shell, ch 5, skip next ch-5 space, tr in next tr, [ch 1, tr in next tr] 8 times, ch 5, skip next ch-5 space, shell in ch-3 space of next shell; rep from * around, omitting last shell, end with Cl in same space as beginning, ch 1, hdc in next ch following beginning cluster.

Rnd 29: Beg-Cl, *ch 6, skip next ch-4 space, tr in next tr, ch 2, skip next ch-2 space, tr in next tr, ch 6, skip next ch-4 space, shell in ch-3 space of next shell, ch 5, skip next (ch-5 space and tr), sc in next ch-1 space, [ch 4, skip next tr, sc in next ch-1 sp] 7 times, ch 5, skip next ch-5 space, shell in ch-3 space of next shell; rep from * around, omitting last shell, end with Cl in same space as beginning, ch 1, hdc in next ch following beginning cluster.

Rnd 30: Beg-Cl, *ch 6, skip first 3 ch of next ch-6 space, tr in next ch, ch 2, skip remaining 2 ch of ch-6 space, tr in next tr, ch 2, skip next ch-2 space, tr in next tr, ch 2, skip first 2 ch of next ch-6 space, tr in next ch, ch 6, skip remaining 3 ch of ch-6 space, shell in ch-3 space of next shell, ch 5, skip next ch-5 space, sc in next ch-4 space, [ch 4, sc in next ch-4 sp] 6 times, ch 5, skip next ch-5 space, shell in ch-3 space of next shell; rep from * around, omitting last shell, end with Cl in same space as beginning, ch 1, hdc in next ch following beginning cluster.

Rnd 31: Beg-Cl, *ch 6, skip next ch-6 space, tr in next tr, [ch 2, skip next ch-2 space, tr in next tr] 3 times, ch 6, skip next ch-6 space, shell in ch-3 space of next shell, ch 5, skip next ch-5 space, sc in next ch-4 space, [ch 4, sc in next ch-4 sp] 5 times, ch 5, skip next ch-5 space, shell in ch-3 space of next shell; rep from * around, omitting last shell, end with Cl in same space as beginning, ch 1, hdc in next ch following beginning cluster.

Rnd 32: Beg-Cl, *ch 6, skip first 3 ch of next ch-6 space, tr in next ch, ch 2, skip remaining 2 ch of ch-6 space, tr in next tr, [ch 2, skip next ch-2 space, tr in next tr] 3 times, ch 2, skip first 2 ch of next ch-6 space, tr in next ch, ch 6, skip remaining 3 ch of ch-6 space, shell in ch-3 space of next shell, ch 5, skip next ch-5 space, sc in next ch-4 space, [ch 4, sc in next ch-4 sp] 4 times, ch 5, skip next ch-5 space, shell in ch-3 space of next shell; rep from

* around, omitting last shell, end with Cl in same space as beginning, ch 1, hdc in next ch following beginning cluster.

Rnd 33: Beg-Cl, *ch 6, skip next ch-6 space, tr in next tr, [ch 2, skip next ch-2 space, tr in next tr] 5 times, ch 6, skip next ch-6 space, shell in ch-3 space of next shell, ch 5, skip next ch-5 space, sc in next ch-4 space, [ch 4, sc in next ch-4 sp] 3 times, ch 5, skip next ch-5 space, shell in ch-3 space of next shell; rep from * around, omitting last shell, end with Cl in same space as beginning, ch 1, hdc in next ch following beginning cluster.

Rnd 34: Beg-Cl, *ch 6, skip first 3 ch of next ch-6 space, tr in next ch, ch 2, skip remaining 2 ch of ch-6 space, tr in next tr, [ch 2, skip next ch-2 space, tr in next tr] 5 times, ch 2, skip first 2 ch of next ch-6 space, tr in next ch, ch 6, skip remaining 3 ch of ch-6 space, shell in ch-3 space of next shell, ch 5, skip next ch-5 space, sc in next ch-4 space, [ch 4, sc in next ch-4 sp] 2 times, ch 5, skip next ch-5 space, shell in ch-3 space of next shell; rep from * around, omitting last shell, end with Cl in same space as beginning, ch 1, hdc in next ch following beginning cluster.

Rnd 35: Beg-Cl, *ch 6, skip first 3 ch of next ch-6 space, tr in next ch, ch 2, skip remaining 2 ch of ch-6 space, tr in next tr, [ch 2, skip next ch-2 space, tr in next tr] 7 times, ch 2, skip first 2 ch of next ch-6 space, tr in next ch, ch 6, skip remaining

3 ch of ch-6 space, shell in ch-3 space of next shell, ch 5, skip next ch-5 space, sc in next ch-4 space, ch 4, sc in next ch-4 space, ch 5, skip next ch-5 space, shell in ch-3 space of next shell; rep from * around, omitting last shell, end with Cl in same space as beginning, ch 1, hdc in next ch following beginning cluster.

Rnd 36: Beg-Cl, *ch 6, skip next ch-6 space, tr in next tr, [ch 2, skip next ch-2 space, tr in next tr, ch 5, skip next ch-2 space, tr in next tr, ch 2, skip next ch-2 space, tr in next tr] 3 times, ch 6, skip next ch-6 space, shell in ch-3 space of next shell, ch 5, skip next ch-5 space, sc in next ch-4 space, ch 5, skip next ch-5 space, shell in ch-3 space of next shell; rep from * around, omitting last shell, end with Cl in same space as beginning, ch 1, hdc in next ch following beginning cluster.

Rnd 37: Beg-Cl, *ch 6, skip next ch-6 space, tr in next tr, [ch 6, skip next (ch-2 space and tr), skip first 2 ch of next ch-5 space, shell in next ch, ch 6, skip next (tr and ch-2 space), tr in next tr] 3 times, ch 6, skip next ch-6 space, shell in ch-3 space of next shell, skip next (ch-5 space, sc and ch-5 space), shell in ch-3 space of next shell; rep from * around, omitting last shell, end with Cl in same space as beginning, ch 1, hdc in next ch following beginning cluster.

Rnd 38: Beg-Cl, *[(ch 5, sc in next ch-6 space) twice, ch 5, (2 sc, Hanging Picot, 2 sc) in ch-3 space of next shell] 3 times, [ch 5, sc in next ch-6 sp] twice, ch 5**, tr6tog cluster over ch-3 spaces of next 2 shells, Attached Picot in top of cluster just made; rep from * around, ending last rep at **, end with Cl in same space as beginning, Attached Picot in top of cluster just made, Sl st in next ch following beginning cluster, fasten off.

Drawstring Waistband

Return to chain edge of Foundation, RS facing. This foundation has height. You have already connected the sc edge; now before continuing with the waist-band, connect the chain edge. Thread the beginning yarn tail coming out of the marked first chain, loop it through two strands of the last chain of the foundation, insert needle down through the marked first chain and first sc. Weave in end.

With RS facing, join yarn with Sl st in marked first chain of foundation.

Rnd 1 (RS): Ch 1, sc in same ch, sc in each chain around, end with Sl st in beginning sc. (108 [120, 132, 144] sc)

Rnd 2 (RS): Ch 2, (dc2tog, ch 3, dc3tog) for beginning V in first sc, [skip next 3 sc, (dc3tog, ch 3, dc3tog) for V in next sc] around, skip last 3 sc, end with Sl st in next ch 1 following beginning cluster. (27 [30, 33, 36] ch-3 spaces)

Rnd 3 (RS): Ch 1, 4 sc in each ch-3 space around, join with Sl st in first sc. (108 [120, 132, 144] sc. Fasten off.

Weave in ends. Block skirt to finished measurements.

String

This technique creates a sturdy, weightier yet flexible braided drawstring with a finer yarn. Keep the stitches relaxed and even. If you crochet too tightly you will not be able to easily locate the bump or strands to be worked.

First St: Begin with a slip knot, ch 2, sc in 2nd ch from hook.

Second St: Turn the sc as you would the page of a book, from right to left. If you trace the top loops of the first sc made, there is a bump, a strand, at the base of the loops. Insert hook from top to bottom (right to left) in the strand, yo and draw up a loop, yo and draw through 2 loops on hook (sc made).

Third St: Turn the piece as you would the page of a book, from right to left. If you trace the top loops of the previous sc made, there is a bump, 2 strands, at the base of the loops. Insert hook from top to bottom (right to left) in the 2 strands, yo and draw up a loop, yo and draw through 2 loops on hook (sc made).

Repeat Third St for length of string desired, or approximately 45 (48, 51, 54)" (114.5 [122, 129.5, 137] cm) (skirt waist plus 18" [45.5 cm]). Weave in ends. Thread string in and out of the waistband in the spaces between the cluster V's, going under one V, then over the next V.

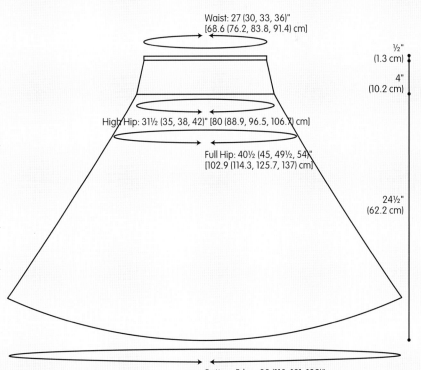

Waist: 27 (30, 33, 36)"
[68.6 (76.2, 83.8, 91.4) cm]

½"
(1.3 cm)

4"
(10.2 cm)

High Hip: 31½ (35, 38, 42)" [80 (88.9, 96.5, 106.7) cm]

Full Hip: 40½ (45, 49½, 54)"
[102.9 (114.3, 125.7, 137) cm]

24½"
(62.2 cm)

Bottom Edge: 99 (110, 121, 132)"
[251.5 (279, 307, 335) cm]

Skill Level
Intermediate

Yarn
Aunt Lydia's Bamboo Crochet
Thread, size 10; 100% viscose
from bamboo; 300 yds (274 m);
#240 Buttercup: 4 (5, 5) balls

lacy layers skirt

Skirts are always in fashion and always on the runways. This fun, flirty skirt, crocheted in Aunt Lydia's Bamboo Crochet Thread, is incredibly soft and yet structured at the same time. I love the way the tiers work up in this crochet thread! Made by working one layer over the next, this is the kind of girly skirt that any woman would love to wear. The Lacy Layers Skirt is a classic wardrobe piece that is a mainstay of any fashionable woman's wardrobe.

Designed by
Shannon
Mullett-Bowlsby

Hook
Steel crochet hook size 7 (1.5 mm)

Gauge
51 sts = 5 ¼" (13.5 cm); 20 rows = 4½" (11.5 cm) in Small Fan pattern

50 sts = 6" (15 cm); 14 rows = 4" (10 cm) in Large Fan pattern

62 sts = 7" (18 cm); 21 rows = 3½" (9 cm) in sc

Notions
Yarn needle

1½" (38 mm) elastic (for waist-band, waist measurement plus 1" (2.5 cm) long

Finished Sizes
Women's sizes S (M, L)

To fit waist size: 26½ (30, 34)" (67.5 [76, 86.5] cm)

Finished waist: 26½ (30, 34)" (67.5 [76, 86.5] cm)

Finished hip: 35½ (40, 45½)" (90 [101.5, 115.5] cm)

Finished length: 22½" (57 cm) adjustable

Reduced Sample of Large Fan Pattern
B

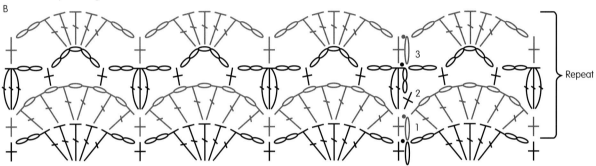

Repeat

Reduced Sample of Small Fan Pattern
A

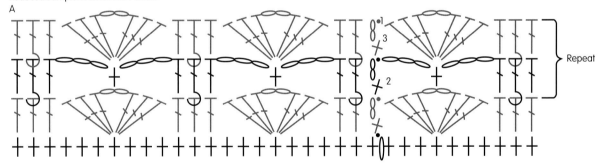

Repeat

NOTES

1. Skirt begins at waistband. Waistband is worked back and forth in rows. The first row of the skirt is worked across one long edge of the waistband.

2. Skirt is worked in two stages. First an underskirt is worked from the waistband down to the hem. Layers of lace are then worked over the lower part of the underskirt. The layers of lace are duplicates of the corresponding rounds of lace in the underskirt.

3. Join the last stitch of each round with a slip stitch in the first stitch of the same round. When beginning the next round, work the first stitch in the same stitch as the joining slip stitch. If first stitch of a round is a dc, work First-dc (see Special Stitches).

Special Stitches

Beginning Cluster (Beg-Cl): *Sc in first stitch, ch 1, yarn over, insert hook in same stitch, yarn over and draw up a loop, yarn over and draw through 2 loops on hook (2 loops remain on hook), yarn over, insert hook in same stitch, yarn over and draw up a loop, yarn over and draw through 2 loops on hook, yarn over and draw through all 3 loops on hook. Note: Do NOT ch 1 at the beginning of the round.*

Cluster (Cl): *Yarn over, insert hook in indicated stitch, yarn over and draw up a loop, yarn over and draw through 2 loops on hook (2 loops remain on hook), [yarn over, insert hook in same stitch, yarn over and draw up a loop, yarn over and draw through 2 loops on hook] twice, yarn over and draw through all 4 loops on hook.*

First double crochet (First-dc): *Sc in first st, ch 2. Notes: Do NOT ch 1 at the beginning of the round before the sc. Use this stitch, whenever the first stitch of a round is a dc.*

Front Post double crochet (FPdc): *Yarn over, insert hook from front to back and then to front again around post of stitch, yarn over and draw up loop, [yarn over and draw through 2 loops on hook] twice.*

Small Fan (small-fan): *(3 dc, ch 2, 3 dc) in indicated stitch.*

Large Fan (large-fan): *Work 5 dc in indicated stitch.*

Pattern Stitches

Small Fan Pattern (multiple of 10 sts)

Rnd 1: *First-dc, dc in next 2 sts, sk next 3 sts, small-fan in next st, sk next 3 sts, *dc in next 3 sts, sk next 3 sts, small-fan in next st, sk next 3 sts; rep from * around, join with Sl st in first st.*

Rnd 2: *First-dc, FPdc around next st, dc in next st, ch 3, sk next 3 dc, sc in next ch-2 sp, ch 3, sk next 3 dc, *dc in next st, FPdc around next st, dc in next st, ch 3, sk next 3 dc, sc in next ch-2 sp, ch 3, sk next 3 dc; rep from * around, join with Sl st in first st.*

Rnd 3: *First-dc, FPdc around next st, dc in next st, sk next ch-3 sp, small-fan in next sc, sk next ch-3 sp, *dc in next st, FPdc around next st, dc in next st, sk next ch-3 sp, small-fan in next sc, sk next ch-3 sp; rep from * around, join with Sl st in first st.*

Repeat Rounds 2 and 3 for Small Fan pattern.

Large Fan Pattern

Rnd 1: *Ch 1, sc in first st, sk next ch-2 sp, [dc in next dc, ch 1] twice, (dc, ch 1, dc) in next dc, [ch 1, dc in next dc] twice, *sk next ch-2 sp, sc in next sc, sk next ch-2 sp, [dc in next dc, ch 1] twice, (dc, ch 1, dc) in next dc, [ch 1, dc in next dc] twice; rep from * around to last ch-2 sp, sk last ch-2 sp, join with Sl st in first sc.*

Rnd 2: *Beg-Cl, ch 2, sk next ch-1 sp, sc in next ch-1 sp, ch 5, sk next ch-1 sp, sc in next ch-1 sp, *ch 2, sk next ch-1 sp, Cl in next sc, ch 2, sk next ch-1 sp, sc in next ch-1 sp, ch 5, sk next ch-1 sp, sc in next ch-1 sp; rep from * around to last ch-1 sp, ch 2, sk last ch-1 sp, join with Sl st in first st.*

Rnd 3: *Ch 1, sc in Beg-Cl, ch 2, sk next ch-2 sp, large-fan in next ch-5 sp, *ch 2, sk next ch-2 sp, sc in next Cl, ch 2, sk next ch-2 sp, large-fan in next ch-5 sp; rep from * around to last ch-2 sp, ch 2, sk last ch-2 sp, join with Sl st in first sc.*

Repeat Rounds 1–3 for Large Fan pattern.

Waistband

Row 1: Work 30 Fsc, turn.

Row 2: Ch 1, sc in first st, sc in back loop only of each st across to last st, sc in last st, turn.

Repeat Row 2 for a total of 158 (180, 204) rows. Piece should measure no more than 26½ (30, 34)" (67.5 [76, 86.5] cm) from beginning. Do not fasten off.

Base Rnd for Skirt (increase): Ch 1, working in ends of rows across long edge of waistband, *2 sc in end of next row, [sc in end of next row, 2 sc in end of next row] twice; rep from * 9 (29, 29) more times, [2 sc in end of next row, sc in end of next row, 2 sc in end of next row] 36 (10, 18) times, turn. (260 [290, 330] sts)

Upper Skirt

Rounds 1–3: Work Rounds 1–3 of Small Fan pattern. (26 [29, 33] small fans)

Rnd 4 (increase): *2 dc in next dc, FPdc around next dc, 2 dc in next dc, ch 3, sk next 3 dc, sc in next ch-2 sp, ch 3, sk next 3 dc, [dc in next st, FPdc around next st, dc in next st, ch 3, sk next 3 dc, sc in next ch-2 sp, ch 3, sk next 3 dc] 3 times; rep from * 2 (2, 3) more times, [3 dc in next st, FPdc around next st, 3 dc in next st, ch 3, sk next 3 dc, sc in next ch-2 sp, ch 3, sk next 3 dc, [dc in next st, FPdc around next st, dc in next st, ch 3, sk next 3 dc, sc in next ch-2 sp, ch 3, sk next 3 dc] 3 times] 0 (1, 0) time(s), **2 dc in next st, FPdc around next st, 2 dc in next st, ch 3, sk next 3 dc, sc in next ch-2 sp, ch 3, sk next 3 dc, [dc in next st, FPdc around next st, dc in next st, ch 3, sk next 3 dc, sc in next ch-2 sp, ch 3, sk next 3 dc] 3 times; rep from ** 2 (2, 3) more times, [dc in next st, FPdc around next st, dc in next st, ch 3, sk next 3 dc, sc in next ch-2 sp, ch 3, sk next 3 dc] 2 (1, 1) time(s), join with Sl st in first st. (272 [306, 346] sts) Note: Count every sc, dc, post st, and chain.

Rnd 5: *Dc in each st to next FPdc, FPdc around next st, dc in each st to next ch-3 sp, sk next ch-3 sp, small-fan in next sc, sk next ch-3 sp; rep from * around, join with Sl st in first st.

Rnd 6: *Dc in each st to next FPdc, FPdc around next st, dc in each st to next small-fan, ch 3, sk next 3 dc, sc in next ch-2 sp, ch 3, sk next 3 dc; rep from * around, join with Sl st in first st.

Rnd 7: Repeat Rnd 5.

Rnd 8 (increase): *Dc in each st to 1 st before next FPdc, 2 dc in next st, FPdc around next st, 2 dc in next st, dc in each dc to next small-fan, ch 3, sk next 3 dc, sc in next ch-2 sp, ch 3, sk next 3 dc, [dc in each st to next FPdc, FPdc around next FPdc, dc in each dc to next small-fan, ch 3, sk next 3 dc, sc in next ch-2 sp, ch 3, sk next 3 dc] 3 times; rep from * 5 (6, 7) more times, [dc in each dc to next FPdc, FPdc around next FPdc, dc in each st to next small-fan, ch 3, sk next 3 dc, sc in next ch-2 sp, ch 3, sk next 3 dc] 2 (1, 1) time(s), join with Sl st in first st. (284 [320, 362] sts)

Rounds 9–28: Repeat Rounds 5–8 five times. (344 [390, 442] sts)

Rounds 29–32: Repeat Rounds 5 and 6 twice.

Upper skirt should measure about 7" (18 cm) from lower edge of waistband.

Lower Underskirt

Notes: When working Rnd 1, work into each st and ch of the previous round.

Rnd 1 (Set-Up): Ch 1, sc in first st, ch 2, sk next 1 (4, 5) sts, large-fan in next st, *ch 2, sk next 4 sts, sc in next st, ch 2, sk next 4 sts, large-fan in next st; rep from * around to last 1 (4, 5) sts, ch 2, sk last 1 (4, 5) sts, join with Sl st in first sc. (35 [39, 44] large fans)

Rounds 2–47: Work in Large Fan pattern for 46 rows. Note: The last rnd you work should be a Rnd 1 of the pattern.

Lower skirt should measure about 14" (35.5 cm), from lower edge of upper skirt. Fasten off.

Overskirt

Notes:

1. Layers are added by working duplicate rounds of lace over the rounds of the lower underskirt.

2. Each layer is worked from the RS and begins with a duplicate round worked into the stitches of a round of the lower underskirt. For example, the first layer begins by working a copy of Rnd 33 of the lower underskirt, inserting the hook into the same stitches (of Rnd 32) as the original Rnd 33, then Rounds 34–41 are worked into the first round of the layer (but, not into any stitches of the underskirt) so that the layer hangs freely and forms a layer on the outside of the skirt.

Layer 1

With RS of skirt facing, insert hook in same st as joining Sl st of Rnd 32. Working into the same sts of Rnd 32, work Rnd 33 of the lower underskirt (this should be Rnd 2 of Large Fan pattern). Working in stitches of the previous round, taking care not to insert hook into the underskirt, work Rounds 34–41 of the lower underskirt. Fasten off.

Layer 2

Work in same manner as layer 1, working duplicates of Rounds 27–35 of lower underskirt.

Layer 3

Work in same manner as layer 1, working duplicates of Rounds 21–29 of lower underskirt.

Layer 4

Work in same manner as layer 1, working duplicates of Rounds 15–23 of lower underskirt.

Layer 5

Work in same manner as layer 1, working duplicates of Rounds 9–17 of lower underskirt.

Layer 6

Work in same manner as layer 1, working duplicates of Rounds 3–11 of lower underskirt.

Finishing

Weave in ends.

Waistband

Cut a piece of 1½" (38 mm) elastic to the waist measurement plus 1" (2.5 cm) for overlap. Place the elastic in the waistband and fold the band over the elastic toward the inside, for sewing. Sew the waistband in place making sure that the stitches do not show on the outside. Before completing the seam, overlap the ends of the elastic and sew them together securely. Use the locking mattress stitch to secure the rest of the waistband opening.

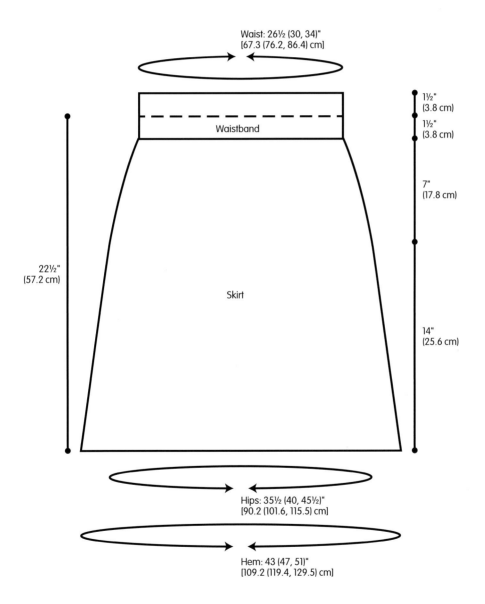

Waist: 26½ (30, 34)"
[67.3 (76.2, 86.4) cm]

1½"
(3.8 cm)

Waistband

1½"
(3.8 cm)

7"
(17.8 cm)

22½"
(57.2 cm)

Skirt

14"
(25.6 cm)

Hips: 35½ (40, 45½)"
[90.2 (101.6, 115.5) cm]

Hem: 43 (47, 51)"
[109.2 (119.4, 129.5) cm]

fashion accents

arielle ruffle bolero
84

catawba lacy shrug
90

venus racer-back tank
94

riviera shorts
98

flame scarf
104

modern waves necklace
108

circles in the sand neckpiece
112

plaid wristlet purse
116

fabulous frills ruffle bag
122

Skill Level

Intermediate

Yarn

Cascade 220 Fingering yarn,
100% Peruvian Highland Wool,
273 yd (250 m), 1.75 oz (50 g):
3 (3, 4) skeins of #2414 Ginger
(A), 1 skein each of #7824 Jack 0
Lantern (B) and #7825 Orange
Sherbert (C)

arielle ruffle bolero

Bold ruffles and a splashy crocheted corsage distinguish this bolero from any ordinary wrap. Wear it to add a splash of whimsy and color over a simple dress. I used a lightweight wool yarn, in highly contrasting colors for impact. You will surely turn heads and get many compliments whenever you wear it.

Designed by
Margaret Hubert

Hook	Gauge	Notions	Finished Sizes
4/E (3.5 cm)	20 sts and 16 rows hdc = 4" (10 cm)	Yarn needle Stitch markers	Women's sizes S (M, L) Finished bust: 34 (36, 38)" (86.5 [91.5, 96.5] cm) Finished length: 16 (16½, 17½)" (40.5 [42, 44.5] cm) This is a close fitting garment that is meant to hug the shoulders and not quite meet in the center.

Special Stitches

Hdc2tog: *Yo, insert hook in next st, yo, draw yarn through st, yo, draw yarn through 2 loops on hook, yo, insert hook in next st, yo, draw yarn through st, yo, draw yarn through 4 loops on hook.*

Reverse sc: *Working from left to right, insert hook in next st to the right, yo, draw yarn through st, yo, draw yarn through 2 loops on hook.*

Back

With A, ch 90 (95,100).

Foundation Row: Hdc in 4th ch from hook and in each ch across, turn. (87 [92, 97] hdc)

Row 1: Ch 3 (counts as hdc here and throughout), skip first hdc, hdc in each hdc across row, hdc in top of turning ch, turn.

Rep Row 1 until piece measures 3½" (9 cm) from the beginning.

Armhole Shaping

Row 1: Sl st over next 5 (5, 6) hdc, ch 3, hdc in each hdc across to within last 5 (5, 6), turn, leaving remaining sts unworked. (77 [82, 85] hdc)

Row 2 (decrease row): Ch 3, hdc2tog, hdc in each hdc across to within last 3 sts, hdc2otg, hdc in top of turning ch, turn. (75 [80, 83] hdc)

Row 3: Ch 3, skip first hdc, hdc in each st across, turn.

Rep Rows 2–3 (3 [4, 4] times). (69 [72, 75] hdc at end of last row)

Work even in hdc until armhole measures 8½ (9, 9½)" (21.5 [23, 24] cm) from beginning. Fasten off.

Left Front

With A, ch 6 (8, 10).

Foundation Row: Hdc in 4th ch from hook and in each ch across, turn. (4 [6, 8] hdc)

Row 1 (increase row): Ch 3, skip first hdc, 2 hdc in next hdc (inc made), hdc in each st across, turn. (5 [7, 9] hdc)

Row 2 (increase row): Ch 3, skip first hdc, hdc in each hdc across to within last 3 sts, 2 hdc next hdc, 1 hdc in top of turning ch, turn. Place a marker here for front edge. (6 [8, 10] hdc)

Row 3–12: Work in hdc, increasing 1 hdc in the second st in from front edge on marked side every row until 15 (17, 19) hdc are on work, turn. (15 [17, 19] hdc)

Work even in hdc until piece measures 3 (3, 3½)" from beginning, ending with a RS row.

Armhole Shaping

Row 1: Sl st over next 5 (5, 6) hdc, ch 3, work hdc in each of next 9 (11, 12) hdc, 2 hdc in next hdc, hdc in top of turning ch, turn. (10 [12, 13] hdc)

Continue to work in hdc, increasing 1 hdc at front edge as established every row, and at the same time, decreasing 1 hdc at armhole edge every other row, 4 (5, 5) times. When armhole decreases are completed, continue increasing at front edge as established until 22 (24, 26) hdc are on work.

Work even for 2 rows, then decreasing 1 hdc at front edge every row until 9 (10, 11) hdc remain. Work even until armhole measures same as back to shoulder. Fasten off.

Right Front

With A, ch 6 (8, 10).

Foundation Row: Hdc in 4th ch from hook and in each ch across, turn. (4 [6, 8] hdc)

Row 1 (increase row): Ch 3, skip first hdc, hdc in each hdc across to within last 3 sts, 2 hdc next hdc, 1 hdc in top of turning ch, turn. (5 [7, 9] hdc)

Row 2 (increase row): Ch 3, skip first hdc, 2 hdc in next hdc (inc made), hdc in each st across, turn. Place a marker here for front edge. (6 [8, 10] hdc)

Row 3–12: Work in hdc, increasing 1 hdc in the second st in from front edge on marked side every row until 15 (17, 19) hdc are on work, turn. (15 [17, 19] hdc)

Work even in hdc until piece measures 3 (3, 3½)" from beginning, ending with a RS row.

Armhole Shaping

Row 1: Ch 3, 2 hdc in next hdc, hdc in each hdc across to within last 5 (5, 6) sts, turn, leaving remaining sts unworked. (10 [12, 13] hdc)

Continue to work in hdc, increasing 1 hdc at Front edge as established every row, and at the same time, decreasing 1 hdc at armhole edge every other row, 4 (5, 5) times. When armhole decreases are completed, continue increasing at front edge as established until 22 (24, 26) hdc are on work.

Work even for 2 rows, then decrease 1 hdc at front edge every row until 9 (10, 11) hdc remain. Work even until armhole measures same as back to shoulder. Fasten off.

Sew shoulder seams. Sew side seams.

Body Ruffle

Rnd 1: With RS facing, join A at right side seam, ch 3, work 4 (6, 8) hdc across bottom of right front, work 5 hdc in corner st, working in row-end sts, work 90 (92, 94) hdc evenly spaced across right front edge to shoulder, work 51 (52, 53) hdc evenly spaced across back neck, work 90 (92, 94) hdc evenly spaced from left shoulder to bottom left front, work 5 hdc in corner st, work 4 (6, 8) hdc evenly spaced across left front bottom edge to seam, work 87 (92, 97) hdc evenly spaced across back bottom edge, join with Sl st in top of beginning ch-3. (338 [352, 399] hdc)

Rnd 2 (increase rnd): Ch 3, [1 hdc in each of the next 9 hdc, 2 hdc in next hdc] 33 (35, 36) times, 1 hdc in each of the last 7 (1, 5) hdc, join with Sl st in top of beginning ch-3. (371 [387, 402] hdc

Rnd 3–4: Ch 3, hdc in each hdc around join with Sl st in top of beginning ch-3.

Rnd 5 (increase rnd): Ch 3, [hdc in each of the next 10 hdc, 2 hdc in next hdc] 33 (35, 36) times, hdc in each of the last 7 (1, 5) hdc, join with a sl st to 3rd ch of beg ch-3. (404 [422, 439] hdc)

Rnd 6–7: Rep Rnd 3.

Rnd 8 (increase rnd): Ch 3, [hdc in each of the next 11 hdc, 2 hdc in next hdc] 33 (35, 36) times, hdc in each of the last 7 (1, 5) hdc, join with Sl st in top of beginning ch-3. (437 [457, 474] hdc)

Rnds 9-10: Rep Rnd 3.

Rnd 11 (increase rnd): Ch 3, [hdc in each of the next 9 hdc, 2 hdc in next hdc] 43 (45, 47) times, hdc in each of the next 6 (6, 3) hdc, join with Sl st in top of beginning ch-3. (480 [502, 521] hdc)

Rnds 12–16: Rep Rnd 3. Fasten off.

Ruffle Edging

Row 1: With RS facing, join A in last rnd of body ruffle below right front side seam, ch 1, sc evenly across right front, across neck edge and down left front edge to bottom edge below left side seam, do not turn.

Row 2: Ch 1, reverse sc in each sc across. Fasten off.

Armhole Ruffle

Before starting place a marker halfway from underarm seam to shoulder seam on each side of armhole.

Rnd 1: With RS facing, join yarn at underarm seam on 1 armhole opening, ch 1, work 18 (19, 20) sc evenly spaced across to first marker, work 18 (19, 20) sc evenly spaced across to shoulder seam, work 18 (19, 20) sc evenly spaced across to next marker, work 18 (19, 20) sc evenly spaced across to underarm seam, join with Sl st in first sc. (72 [76, 80] sc).

Rnd 2: Ch 1, sc in each of the first 19 (20, 21) sc, 2 hdc in each of the next 34 (36, 38) sc, sc in each of the next 19 (20, 21) sc, join with Sl st in first sc. (34 [36, 38] hdc; 38 [40, 42] sc)

Rnd 3: Ch 1, sc in each of the first 18 (19, 20) sc, [hdc in next hdc, 2 hdc in next hdc] 35 (37, 39) times, sc in each of the next 18 (19, 20) sc, join with Sl st in first sc. hdc (18 [19, 20] sc each side), join with Sl st in first sc. (105 [111, 117] hdc; 36 [38, 40] sc)

Rnd 4: Ch 1, sc in each of the first 18 (19, 20) sc, [hdc in each of next 2 hdc, 2 hdc in next hdc] 35 (37, 39) times, sc in each of the last 18 (19, 20) sc, join with Sl st in first sc. (140 [148, 156] hdc; 36 [38, 40] sc)

Rnds 5–7: Ch 1, sc in each of the first 18 (19, 20) sc, hdc in each of next 140 (148, 156) hdc, 1 sc in each of the last 18 (19, 20) sc, join with Sl st in first sc. (140 [148, 156] hdc; 36 [38, 40] sc)

Embellishments

Poppy

(Make 2)

Outer Petal

With B, ch 5, join with a Sl st to form a ring.

Rnd 1: Ch 1, 8 sc in ring, join with Sl st in first sc. (8 sc)

Rnd 2: Ch 3 (counts as dc here and throughout), *2 dc in next sc**, dc in next sc; rep from * around, ending last rep at **, join with Sl st in top of beginning ch-3. (12 dc)

Rnd 3: Ch 3, dc in first st, 2 dc in each dc around, join with Sl st in top of beginning ch-3. (24 dc)

Rnd 4: Ch 3, skip first st, *2 dc next dc**, dc next dc; rep from * around, ending last rep at **, join with Sl st in top of beginning ch-3. (36 dc)

Rnd 5: Ch 3, skip first st, dc in next dc, *2 dc in next dc**, dc in each of next 2 dc; rep from * around, ending last rep at **, join with Sl st in top of beginning ch-3. (48 dc)

Rnd 6: Ch 3, skip first st, dc in next 2 dc, *2 dc in next dc**, dc in each of next 3 dc; rep from * around, ending last rep at **, join with Sl st in top of beginning ch-3. (60 dc)

Rnd 7: Ch 1, sc in first 2 sts, *hdc in next dc, dc in each of the next 4 dc, hdc in next dc**, sc in each of the next 4 dc; rep from * around, ending last rep at **, sc in each of last 2 dc, join with Sl st in top of beginning ch-3. (6 scallops)

Rnd 8: *Ch 3, sc in next st; rep from * around, join with Sl st to base of beg ch-3. Fasten off.

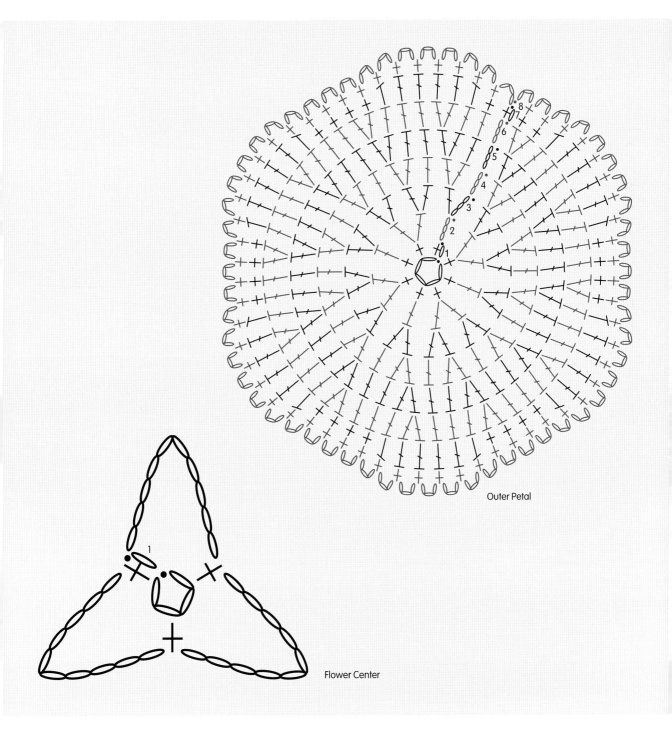

Outer Petal

Flower Center

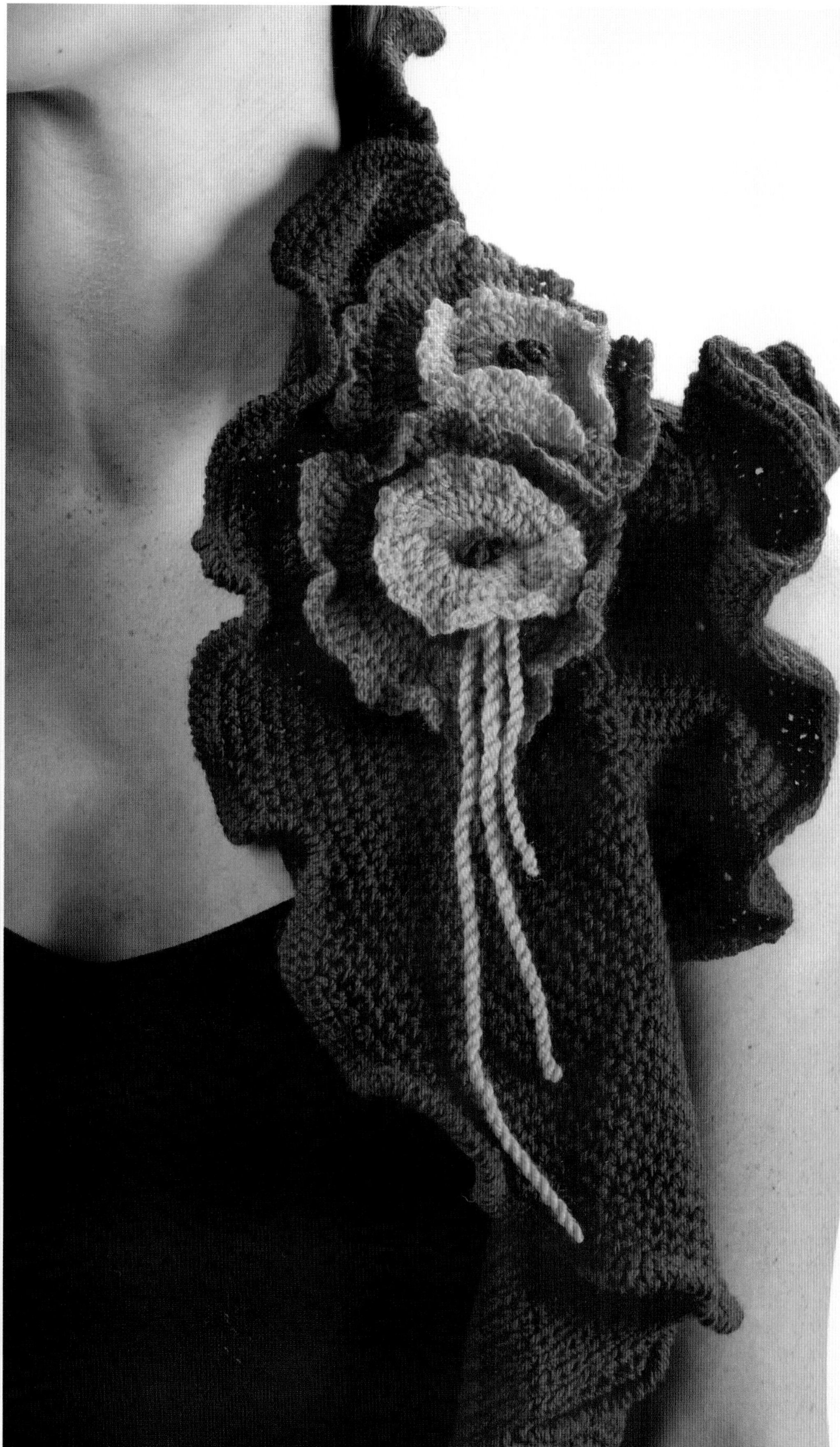

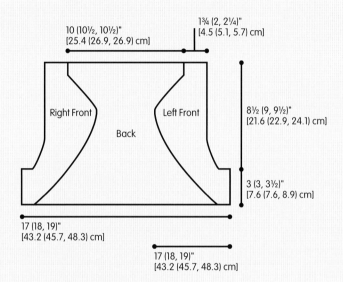

10 (10½, 10½)"
[25.4 (26.9, 26.9) cm]

1¾ (2, 2¼)"
[4.5 (5.1, 5.7) cm]

Right Front

Left Front

Back

8½ (9, 9½)"
[21.6 (22.9, 24.1) cm]

3 (3, 3½)"
[7.6 (7.6, 8.9) cm]

17 (18, 19)"
[43.2 (45.7, 48.3) cm]

17 (18, 19)"
[43.2 (45.7, 48.3) cm]

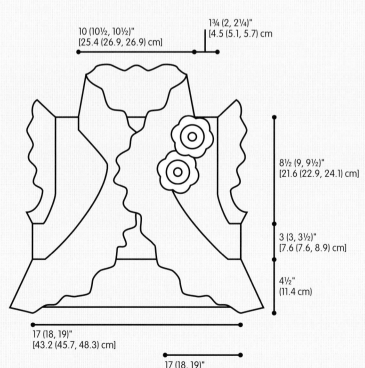

10 (10½, 10½)"
[25.4 (26.9, 26.9) cm]

1¾ (2, 2¼)"
[4.5 (5.1, 5.7) cm

8½ (9, 9½)"
[21.6 (22.9, 24.1) cm]

3 (3, 3½)"
[7.6 (7.6, 8.9) cm]

4½"
(11.4 cm)

17 (18, 19)"
[43.2 (45.7, 48.3) cm]

17 (18, 19)"
[43.2 (45.7, 48.3) cm]

Second Petal

With B, work same as outer petal through Rnd 4.

Rnd 5: Rep Rnd 8 of outer petal. Fasten off.

Center

With A, ch 4, join with a Sl st to form a ring.

Rnd 1: [Ch 10, sc in ring] 3 times. Fasten off leaving a 6" (15 cm) sewing length.

Finishing

Place second petal on top of outer petal, place center on top of both petals and using sewing length, sew all 3 layers together. Rep with second flower. Sew flowers in place on sweater as pictured.

Twisted Cord

(Make 1 in each designated length)
Cut 2 strands of A, 24" (61 cm) long. Cut 2 strands of A, 36" (91.5 cm) long. Cut 2 strands of A, 48" (122 cm) long. Fold in 2 matching strands in half, anchoring the folded end, twist and twist these 2 strands until they become very tightly wound. Being sure not to let go of ends, bring both cut end and folded end together, hold up and allow to twist into a cord. Tie loose end tightly, near the end. Rep for remaining strands, making a total of 3 twisted cords, Attach between outer petal and second petal of lower flower, hanging down.

Blocking not recommended for ruffle. If body needs blocking, place garment on a padded surface, sprinkle lightly with water, pat body into shape, allow to dry.

Skill Level

Intermediate

Yarn

Bijou Basin Ranch Tibetan Dream sock yarn; 85% yak down, 15% nylon; 440 yds (403 m)/4 oz (113 g); #02 Natural Cream: 2 hanks

catawba lacy shrug

Just enough warmth and beautiful texture is what you'll get with this lacy shrug. Wear it on late summer evenings when it's just cool enough for a cover but not cool enough for a coat. The cuffs and shoulder shaping helps the shrug stay in place without tugging. The lacy fabric makes the shrug elegant and interesting.

Designed by Ellen Gormley

Hook	**Gauge**	**Notions**	**Finished Size**
5/F (3.75 mm)	9 sc = 2" (5 cm) in cuff pattern	Tapestry needle	Women's sizes S (M)
	1 motif, blocked = 5" (12.5 cm)		Width from cuff to cuff: 55 (65)" (140 [165] cm)
			Width across back: 30 (35)" (76 [89] cm)

Notes

Make and join 46 (54) motifs and 4 half motifs while completing last rnd, following assembly diagram for placement, making sure to join sleeves across bottom edges.

Special Stitches

Beginning cluster (Beg-Cl): Ch 3, yo, insert hook in same stitch, yo and draw up a loop, yo and draw through 2 loops on hook (2 loops remain on hook), yo, insert hook in same stitch, yo and draw up a loop, yarn over and draw through 2 loops on hook, yo and draw through all 3 loops on hook.

Cluster (Cl): [Yo, insert hook in next stitch, yo and draw up a loop, yo and draw through 2 loops on hook] 3 times in same stitch, yo and draw through all 4 loops on hook.

First Motif

Ch 4, Sl st in first ch to form a ring.

Rnd 1 (RS): Ch 6 (counts as dc, ch 3), [dc, ch 3] 5 times in ring, join with Sl st in 3rd ch of beg ch-6. (6 dc)

Rnd 2: Ch 1, sc in first st, Sl st in ch-3 space, *Beg-Cl in ch-3 space, ch-4, sc in next dc, ** Sl st in next ch-3 space; rep from * around, ending last rep at **, join with Sl st in first sc.

Rnd 3: Ch 8 (counts as tr, ch 4), *sc in next ch-4 space, ch 4**, tr in next sc; rep from * around, ending last rep at **, sc in 4th ch of beg ch-8. (6 tr, 12 ch-4 spaces)

Rnd 4: Ch 1, sc in first st, *ch 9, sc in next sc, ch 9 **, sc in next tr] 4 times; rep from * around, ending last rep at **, join with Sl st in first sc. Fasten off.

Motif Joined on One Side (2 Loops)

Work same as first motif through Rnd 3

Rnd 4: Ch 1, sc in first st, ch 4, Sl st in ch-9 loop of adjacent motif, ch 4, sc in next sc, ch 4, Sl st in ch-9 space of adjacent motif, ch 4, sc in next tr, *ch 9, sc in next sc, ch 9 **, sc in next tr] 4 times; rep from * around, ending last rep at **, join with Sl st in first sc. Fasten off.

Motif Joined on Two Sides (4 Loops)

Work same as first motif through Rnd 3

Rnd 4: Ch 1, sc in first st, [ch 4, Sl st in ch-9 loop of adjacent motif, ch 4, sc in next sc, ch 4, Sl st in ch-9 space of adjacent motif, ch 4, sc in next tr] twice, *ch 9, sc in next sc, ch 9 **, sc in next tr] 4 times; rep from * around, ending last rep at **, join with Sl st in first sc. Fasten off.

Half Motif

(Two on each wrist end)
Ch 4, Sl st in first ch to form a ring.

Row 1 (WS): Ch 6 (counts as dc, ch 3), [dc, ch 3] twice in ring, dc in ring, turn. (4 dc)

Row 2 (RS): Ch 1, Sl st in ch-3 space, *Beg-Cl in ch-3 space, ch 4**, sc in next dc, Sl st in next ch-3 space; rep from * twice, sc in 4th ch of turning ch, turn. (3 Beg-Cl)

Row 3: Ch 8 (counts as first tr, ch 4), *sc in next ch-4 space, ch 4, tr in next sc**, ch 4; rep from * once, rep from * to ** once, turn. (4 tr, 6 ch-4 spaces)

Row 4: Ch 1, sc in first tr, *ch 4, Sl st in ch-9 space of adjacent motif, ch 4, sc in next sc, ch 4, Sl st in ch-9 space of adjacent motif, ch 4, sc in next tr; rep from * across, joining to 3 motifs. Fasten off.

Wrist Edging

Rnd 1: Join yarn with sc in first ch-4 space of either Half Motif on cuff edge of one sleeve, work 4 more sc in same space, 5 sc in next row-end tr, 3 sc in next row end dc, 2 sc in center ring, 3 sc in next row-end ch-3, 5 sc in next row-end ch-4 spae, 5 dc in each oc nest 2 ch-4 spaces, 6 sc in each of next 2 ch-7 space, 5 sc in each of next 2 ch-4 space; rep from * around, join with Sl st in first sc. (100 sc)

Ribbing

Row 1: Ch 10, sc in 2nd ch from hook and in each ch across, ch 1, skip next 4 sc on wrist edging, Sl st in next sc, turn. (9 sc)

Row 2: Skip next ch-1 space, sc in back loop only of next 9 sc, turn. (9 sc)

Row 3: Ch 1, working in blp only, sc in next 9 sc of cuff, ch 1, skip next 4 sc on wrist edging, Sl st in next sc, turn. (9 sc)

Rows 4–40: Rep rows 2–3 (18 times); then rep Row 2 once. Fasten off leaving a 12" tail. Using yarn needle and yarn tail, matching sts, sew last row to foundation ch of ribbing.

Rep wrist edging and ribbing on cuff edge of other sleeve. Fasten off. Weave in ends.

Assembly
diagram size
small

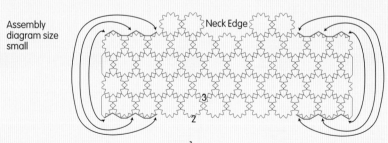

Assembly
diagram size
medium

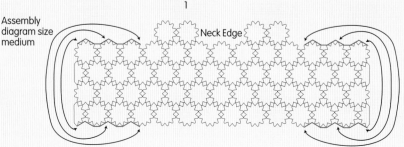

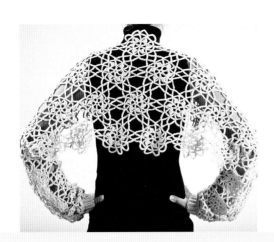

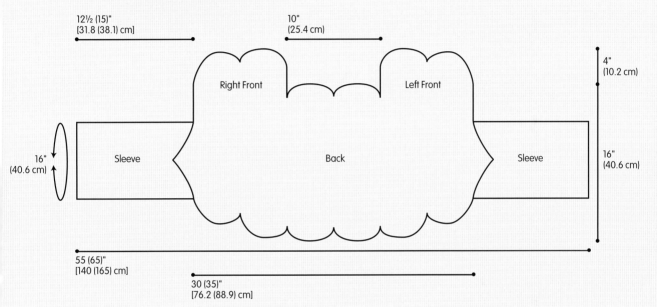

12½ (15)"
[31.8 (38.1) cm]

10"
(25.4 cm)

4"
(10.2 cm)

Right Front

Left Front

16"
(40.6 cm)

Sleeve

Back

Sleeve

16"
(40.6 cm)

55 (65)"
[140 (165) cm]

30 (35)"
[76.2 (88.9) cm]

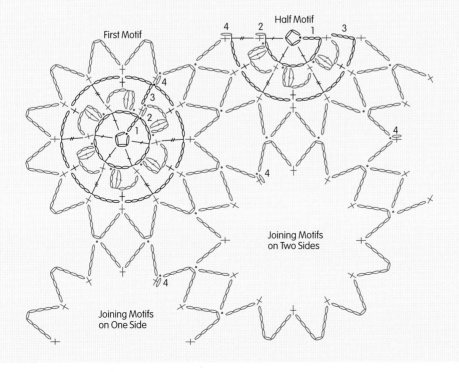

First Motif

Half Motif

Joining Motifs
on Two Sides

Joining Motifs
on One Side

Skill Level
Intermediate

Yarn
Blue Heron yarns Rayon Metallic;
88% rayon, 12% metallic; 550 yd
(503 m)/8 oz (227 g); Carnelian: 2
(2, 3) skeins

venus racerback tank

My love of sports inspired this
racerback tank. The vertical pattern
gives you a lean, long look. It's sporty
enough to wear with jeans or elegant
enough with its sparkling gold flecks
to wear with a black skirt and heels.

Designed by
Sharon Hubert
Valencia

Hooks
5/F (3.75 mm)
6/G (4 mm)

Gauge
18 sts and 8 rows dc in back loop only = 4" (10 cm) with 5/F (3.75 mm) hook

Notions
Yarn needle
Sewing needle and matching sewing thread

Finished Sizes
Women's sizes S (M, L)

Finished bust: 36 (40, 44)" (91.5 [101.5, 112] cm)

Finished length: 22 (22½, 22½)" (56 [57, 57] cm)

This is a very close fitting garment. Fabric is very stretchy and hugs the body.

Note
This sweater is made in 3 pieces. All stitches are worked in back loop only unless otherwise stated.

Special Stitches
Dc2tog: *[Yo, insert hook in next st, yo, draw yarn through st, yo, draw yarn through 2 loops on hook] twice, yo, draw yarn through 3 loops on hook.*

Piece 1
Starting at center front, with 6/G hook, ch 81, change to 5/F hook.

Row 1 (RS): Dc in 3rd ch from hook and in each ch across, turn. (80 dc)

Row 2: Ch 3 (counts as dc here and throughout), skip first dc, dc in back loop of each dc across, ending with 2 dc in top of turning ch (inc made), turn. (81 dc)

Row 3: Ch 3, dc in first st (inc made), dc in back loop only of each dc across, turn. (82 dc)

Row 4: Rep Row 2, do not turn. (84 dc)

Size M and L Only
Rows 5–6: Rep Rows 3–4, do not turn at end of last row. (86 dc)

Size L Only
Rows 7-8: Rep Rows 3–4, do not turn at end of last row. (88 dc)

All Sizes
Strap Section
Note: *The first dc after and the last dc before the sc straps should be in both loops of the dc rather than in the back loop only.*

Row 1: Ch 125 to begin back and strap, turn, dc in 3rd ch from hook, dc in next 67 ch (for back), sc in next 55 ch (for strap), dc in both loops of next dc, dc in back loop of each dc across (for front), turn. (70 dc for back; 55 sc for strap; 85 dc for front)

Row 2: Ch 3, skip first dc, dc in back loop of next 83 dc, dc in both loops of next dc, ch 55, dc in both loops of next dc on back, dc in back loop only of next 69 dc, turn. (85 dc on front; 70 dc on back)

Row 3: Ch 3, skip first dc, dc in back loop only of next 68 dc, dc in both loops of next dc, sc in next 55 ch, dc in both loops of next dc, dc in back loop only of next 84 dc, turn.

Rows 4–7: Rep Rows 2–3 twice.

Shaping Armhole
Row 14: Ch 3, skip first dc, dc in back loop of next 34 dc, sc in back loop of next 25 dc, dc in back loop of next 14 dc, sc in top of turning ch, turn. (49 dc; 26 sc)

Row 15: Ch 2, dc2tog in back loop of next 2 sts, dc in back loop only of next 12 dc, sc in back loop only of next 25 sc, dc in back loop only of next 35 dc, turn.

Row 16: Ch 3, skip first dc, dc in back loop of next 34 dc, sc in back loop of next 25 dc, dc in back loop of next 12 dc, dc2tog in back loop of next 2 sts, turn.

Row 17: Ch 3, dc2tog in back loop of next 2 sts, dc in back loop of next 10 dc, sc in back loop of next 25 sc, dc in back loop of next 35 dc, turn.

Row 18: Ch 3, dc in back loop of next 35 dc, 25 sc, dc in back loop of next 10 dc, dc2tog in back loop of next 2 sts, turn.

Row 19: Ch 3, dc2tog in back loop of next 2 sts, dc in back loop of next 8 dc, sc in back loop of next 25 sc, dc in back loop of next 35 dc, turn.

Row 20: Ch 3, dc in back loop of next 35 dc, sc in back loop of next 25 sc, dc in back loop of next 10 dc, turn.

Row 21: Ch 2, sc in back loop of next 35 sts, dc in back loop of next 35 dc, turn.

Row 22: Ch 3, dc in back loop of next 35 dc, sc in back loop of next 35 sc, turn:

Row 23: Ch 2, sc in back loop of next 35 sc, dc in back loop of next 35 dc, turn.

Row 24: Ch 3, dc in back loop of next 35 dc, sc in back loop of next 35 sc, turn.

Rows 25–28 (30, 32): Ch 3, dc in back loop of next 70 sts. Fasten off.

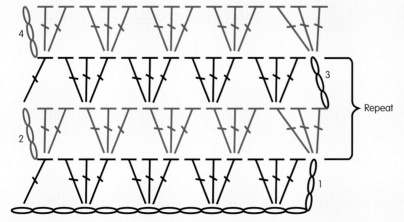

Front Inset Pattern

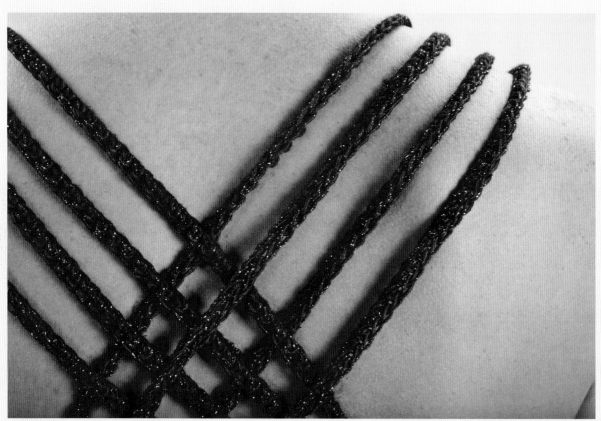

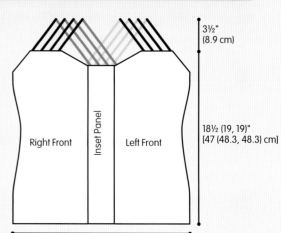

3½"
(8.9 cm)

Right Front

Inset Panel

Left Front

18½ (19, 19)"
[47 (48.3, 48.3) cm]

18 (20, 22)"
[45.7 (50.8, 55.9) cm]

Piece 2

Work same as Piece 1. Row 1 is now a WS row.

Piece 3 (Front Inset)

Starting at neck edge, with 6/G hook, ch 17, change to 5/F hook.

Row 1: 3 dc 5th ch from hook, skip next 2 ch, 3 dc in next ch, skip next 2 ch, 3 dc in next ch, skip next 2 ch, 3 dc in next ch, skip next 2 ch, 1 dc in last ch, turn.

Row 2: Ch 3, 2 dc in first dc, skip next 2 dc, 3 dc in next dc, skip next 2 dc, 3 dc in next dc, skip next 2 dc, 3 dc in next dc, skip next 3 dc, 3 dc in last ch, turn.

Row 3: Ch 3, skip first 2 dc, 3 dc in next dc st, skip 2 dc, 3 dc in next dc st, skip 2 dc, 3 dc in next dc st, skip 2 dc, 3 dc in next dc st, skip 2 dc, 1 dc in last ch, turn.

Row 4–38: Rep Rows 2-3 (17 times); then rep Row 2 once. Fasten off.

Note: Compare the length of this piece with the length of the front pieces, you may need to add or subtract a row for a proper fit. This is a very stretchy garment, be sure to lay flat when comparing.

Assembly

Sew center front panel to each front edge of piece one and piece two. Weave one back panel under and over the straps of the other side and sew center back seam. Sew the two side back seams. Weave in ends. Tack straps where they cross in place with a needle and thread.

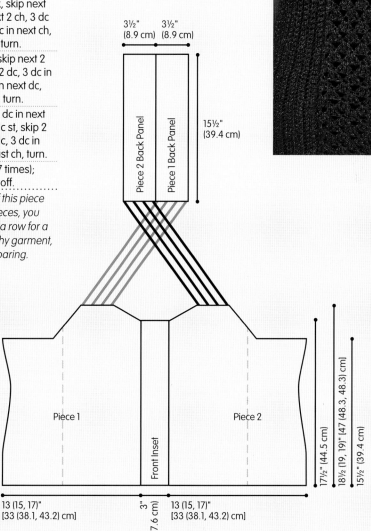

3½" (8.9 cm) 3½" (8.9 cm)

Piece 2 Back Panel

Piece 1 Back Panel

15½" (39.4 cm)

Piece 1

Piece 2

Front Inset

17½" (44.5 cm)

18½ (19, 19)" [47 (48.3, 48.3) cm]

15½" (39.4 cm)

13 (15, 17)" [33 (38.1, 43.2) cm]

3" (7.6 cm)

13 (15, 17)" [33 (38.1, 43.2) cm]

Skill Level	**Yarn**
Intermediate	Tahki Cotton Classic Lite, 100% Mercerized Cotton, 146 yd (135 m), 1.75 oz (50 g), 6 (7, 8) skeins #4002 Black (A); 1 skein each of #4001 White (B), #4870 Dark Bright Blue (C), #4995 Deepest Red (D), #4253 Wheat (E), and #4405 Tangerine (F)

riviera shorts

Designed by
Margaret Hubert

All eyes will turn your way when you wear these cotton shorts. Cool, absorbant cotton yarn drapes beautifully, and the loose fit and black color contrasted with brights is very flattering. Pair the shorts with a silk blouse for an evening out, or pop over a bathing suit when vacationing at your favorite resort.

Hooks	Gauge	Notions	Finished Sizes
4/E (3.5 mm) for size S	With 4/E hook, 1 pattern Rep = 2" (5 cm)	Yarn needle	Women's sizes S (M, L)
5/F (3.75 mm) for size M	With 5/F hook, 1 pattern rep = 2½" (6.5 cm)	2 stitch markers	Finished waist: 27 (34, 40½)" (68.5 [86.5, 103] cm)
6/G (4 mm) for size L	With 6/G hook, 1 pattern rep = 3" (7.5 cm)		Finished hips: 34 (42, 50)" (86.5 [106.5, 127] cm)
			Finished length: 17(19, 20½)" (43 [48.5, 52] cm)

Reduced Sample of Pattern

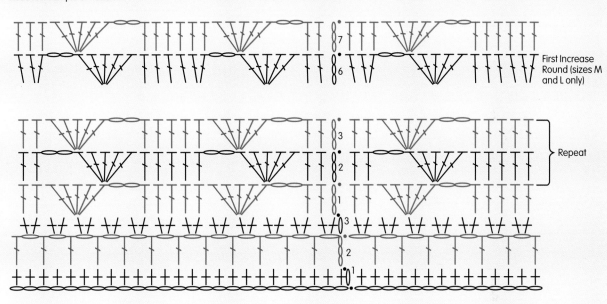

First Increase Round (sizes M and L only)

Repeat

Shorts

Foundation Rnd: With 4/E hook for size S, size 5/F hook for size M, or size 6/G hook for size L, ch 162, being careful not to twist ch, join with a Sl st to form a ring.

Rnd 1: Ch 1, sc in each ch around, join with Sl st in first sc. (162 sc)

Rnd 2: Ch 4 (counts as dc, ch 1), skip first 2 sc, *dc in next sc, ch 1, skip next sc; rep from * around, join with Sl st in 3rd ch of beg ch-4. (81 ch-1 spaces).

Rnd 3: Ch 1, work 2 sc in each ch-1 space around, working 4 increases evenly spaced around, join with Sl st in first sc. (166 sc)

Sizes S and L, change to 5/F hook.

Begin Shell and Rib Pattern

Rnd 1: Ch 3 (counts as dc here and throughout) (seam st), skip first st, dc in each next 2 dc, *ch 2, skip next 4 sc, 5 dc in next sc**, skip next 2 sc, dc in each next 5 sc; rep from * around, ending last rep at **, skip next 2 sc, dc in each next 2 sc, join with Sl st in top of beg ch. (14 groups of 5 dc; 14 shells)

Rnd 2: Ch 3, skip first st, dc in next 2 dc, *skip next ch-2 space, 5 dc in first dc of next shell, ch 2, skip next 4 dc of same shell**, dc in each next 5 dc; rep * around, ending last rep at **, dc in each of last 2 dc, join with Sl st in top of beg ch.

Rnd 3: Ch 3, skip first st, dc in next 2 dc, *ch 2, skip next 4 dc, 5 dc in last dc of same shell, skip next ch-2 space**, dc in each next 5 dc; rep from * around, ending last rep at **, dc in each last 2 dc, join with Sl st in top of beg ch.

Rnds 4–5: Rep Rnds 2–3.

Rnd 6 (inc rnd sizes M and L): Ch 3, skip first st, dc in next 2 dc, *skip next ch-2 space, 5 dc in first dc of next shell, ch 2, skip next 4 dc of same shell, 1 (2, 2) dc in next dc (inc made in sizes M and L only)**, dc in each next 4 dc; rep from * around, ending last rep at **, dc in last dc, join with Sl st in top of beg ch. (14 groups of 5 [6, 6] dc; 14 shells)

Rnds 7-9: Using 5 or F hook for Sm and Med, change to #6 or G for Large size. Continue using these hooks for remainder of garment. Work even in established pattern.

Rnd 10 (inc rnd): Ch 3, dc in next dc, 2 dc in next dc (inc made), *skip next ch-2 space, 5 dc in first dc of next shell, ch 2, skip 4 dc of same shell, dc in each dc to last dc of group**, 2 dc in last dc (inc made); rep from * around, ending last rep at **, join with Sl st in top of beg ch. (14 groups of 6 [7, 7] dc; 14 shells)

Rnds 11–13: Work even in established pattern.

Rnd 14: Ch 3, skip first st, dc in next 2 dc, *skip next ch-2 space, 5 dc in first dc of next shell, ch 2, skip next 4 dc of same shell, 2 dc in next dc (inc made), dc in each dc of group; rep from * around, join with Sl st in top of beg ch. (14 groups of 7 [8, 8] dc; 14 shells)

Rnds 15–30: Repeat Rnds 7-14 twice. (14 groups of 11 [12, 12] dc; 14 shells)

Rnds 31–33: Repeat Rnds 7-9 once. Place a marker in top of second to last dc.

First Leg

Rnd 1 (inc rnd): Ch 3, *dc in each dc to last dc of group, 2 dc in last dc (inc made), skip next ch-2, 5 dc in first dc of next shell, ch 2, skip last 4 dc of same shell; rep from * 6 times, dc in next 5 dc, dc through both the next dc AND the beg ch-3 of last rnd, join with Sl st in top of beg ch. Place a marker in top of next dc. Separation of legs completed.

Rnds 2–4: Work even in established pattern on 7 pattern reps.

Rnd 5 (inc rnd): Ch 3, dc in each dc of rib, *skip next ch-2 space, 5 dc in first dc of next shell, ch 2, skip last 4 dc of same

shell, 2 dc in next dc, dc in each remaining dc of group; rep from * around, join with Sl st in top of beg ch.

Rnd 6: Work even in established pattern. Fasten off.

Second Leg

Rnd 1: With RS facing, join yarn with Sl st in first marked st to the left of first Leg, rep Rnd 1 of first leg, ending with last dc made through the tops of both marked stitches.

Rnd 2–6: Rep Rnds 2–6 of first Leg. Remove markers.

Waist Tie

With 6/G hook and 2 strands of yarn held together as one, make a ch 44 (48, 52)" (112 [127, 132] cm) long. Fasten off.

Embellishments

Note: Work all embellishments with 4/E hook.

Daisy

(Make 3)

With F, ch 4, join with a Sl st to form a ring.

Rnd 1: Ch 3, 13 dc in ring, join with Sl st in top of beg ch, pull up a loop of B, fasten off F. (14 dc).

Petals: With B, *ch 8, Sl st in 2nd ch from hook, sc in next 2 ch, hdc in next 2 ch, dc in next 2 ch, skip next dc in Rnd 1, Sl st in next dc; rep from * around. Fasten off.

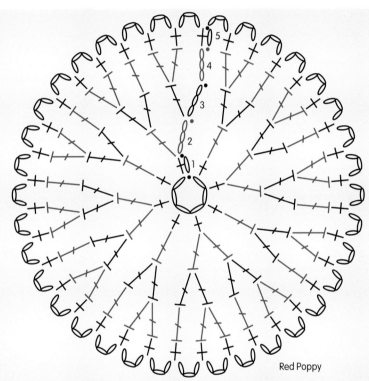

Red Poppy

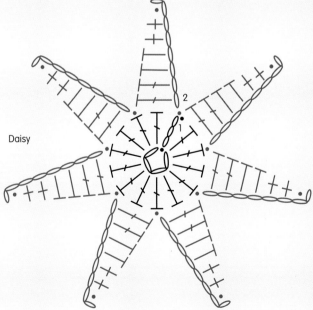

Daisy

Red Poppy

(Make 1)

With F, ch 5, join with a Sl st to form a ring

Rnd 1: Ch 1, 8 sc in ring, join with Sl st in first sc, pull up a loop of A, fasten off F.

Rnd 2: With A, ch 3 (counts as dc here and throughout), dc in first st, *dc in next sc, 2 dc in next sc; rep from * around, join with Sl st in top of beg ch, pull up a loop of D, fasten off A. (12 dc).

Rnd 3: With D, ch 3, dc in first dc, 2 dc in each dc around, join with Sl st in top of beg ch. (24 dc)

Rnd 4: Ch 3, *2 dc next dc**, dc next dc; rep from * around, ending last rep at **, join with Sl st in top of beg ch. (36 dc)

Rnd 5: Ch 1, sc in first st, ch 3, *sc in next sc, ch 3; rep from * around, join with Sl st in first sc. Fasten off leaving a sewing length.

Eight-Petal Flower

(Make 3)

With E, ch 4, join with a Sl st to form a ring.

Rnd 1: Ch 3 (counts as dc), 15 dc in ring, join with Sl st in top of beg ch, pull up a loop of C, fasten off E. (16 dc).

Rnd 2: With C, *ch 7, skip next dc, Sl st in next dc; rep from * around. (8 ch-7 loops)

Rnd 3: [2 sc, 3 hdc, dc, 3 hdc, 2 sc] in each ch-7 loop around, join with Sl st in first sc. Fasten off leaving a sewing length.

Five-Petal Flower

(Make 5 with F, 1 with C, and 1 with E)

Ch 4, join with a Sl st to form a ring.

Rnd 1: Ch 1, 10 sc in ring, join with Sl st in first sc. Fasten off leaving a sewing length.

Rnd 2: *Ch 2, 3 dc in next sc, ch 2, Sl st in next sc; rep from * around. (5 petals) Fasten off leaving a sewing length.

Small Circles

(Make 2 with D)

Ch 4, join with a Sl st to form a ring.

Rnd 1: Ch 1, 10 sc in ring, join with Sl st in first sc. Fasten off leaving a sewing length.

Finishing

Sew flowers to front of shorts as pictured. Weave in ends. Lay garment on a padded surface, pin into shape using rust proof pins, spray lightly with water, allow to dry. Beginning and ending at center front, weave waist tie in and out of ch-1 spaces in Rnd 2 of waistband.

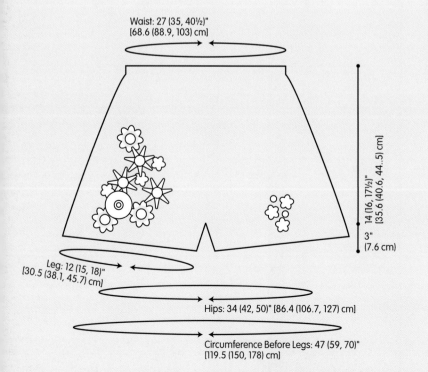

Waist: 27 (35, 40½)"
[68.6 (88.9, 103) cm]

14 [16, 17½)"
[35.6 (40.6, 44..5) cm]

3"
(7.6 cm)

Leg: 12 (15, 18)"
[30.5 (38.1, 45.7) cm]

Hips: 34 (42, 50)" [86.4 (106.7, 127) cm]

Circumference Before Legs: 47 (59, 70)"
[119.5 (150, 178) cm]

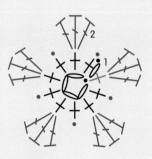

5-Petal Flower

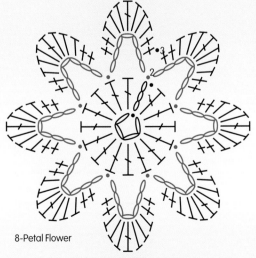

8-Petal Flower

Small Circle

Skill Level
Intermediate

Yarn
Lorna's Laces Shepherd Sport;
100% wool; 200yds (183 m)/2 oz
(50 g); #64 gold hill: 2 hanks

flame scarf

In all ways this scarf is a light. The stitch pattern and yarn both reflect the inspiration of flame. Ever changing and moving, this scarf with its wonderful drape is really something I'd be proud to wear.

Designed by
Ellen Gormley

Hook	Gauge	Notions	Finished Size
5/F (3.75 mm)	24 sts (4 reps) = 5" (12.5 cm); 6 rows = 4" (10 cm) in pattern	Tapestry needle	11½" x 48" (30 x 122 cm)

Reduced Sample of Pattern

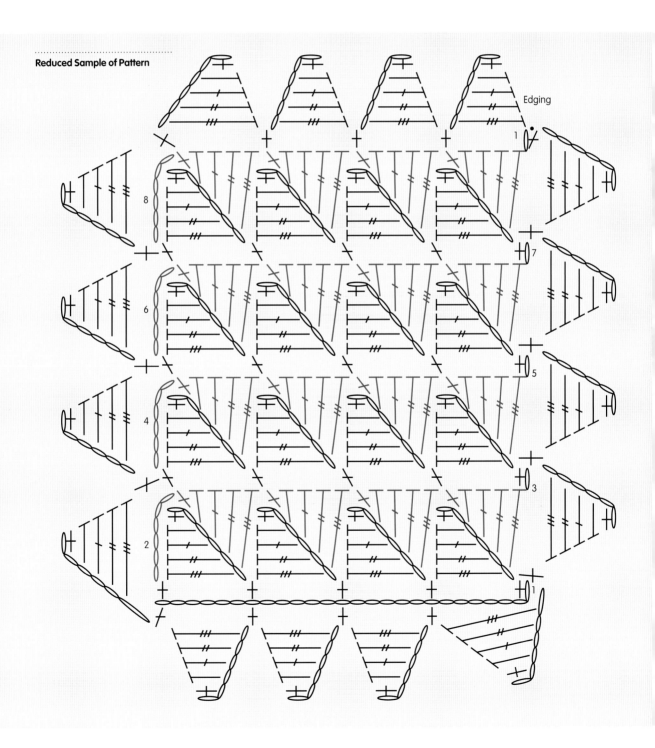

Edging

Scarf

Ch 224.

Row 1 (RS): Sc in 2nd ch from hook, *ch 6, sc in 2nd ch from hook, hdc in next ch, dc in next ch, tr in next ch, dtr in next ch, skip next 5 chs on foundation ch, sc in next ch; rep from * across, turn. (37 rep)

Row 2: Ch 6, working in opposite side of 6 ch of last triangle made, *sc in ch at base of sc, hdc next ch, dc in next ch, tr in next ch, dtr in next ch; rep from * in each triangle across, turn.

Row 3: Ch 1, sc in first dtr, *ch 6, sc in 2nd ch from hook, hdc in next ch, dc in next ch, tr in next ch, dtr in next ch, skip next 4 sts, sc in next sc; rep from * across, turn.

Rows 4–13: Rep rows 2–3 five times.

Row 14: Rep Row 2. Do not fasten off.

Edging

Row 1: Ch 1, sc in first dtr, rotate work to work down the short side toward row 1 of scarf, [ch 6, sc in 2nd ch from hook, hdc in next ch, dc in next ch, tr in next ch, dtr in next ch, skip next row-end dtr, sc in next ch at base of dtr] 6 times across to next corner ending with a sc in ch at base dtr at corner; rotate to work across opposite side of foundation ch of row 1; *ch 6, sc in 2nd ch from hook, hdc in next ch, dc in next ch, tr in next ch, dtr in next ch, skip next 5 chs on foundation ch, sc in next ch at base of sc; rep from * across to corner; [ch 6, sc in 2nd ch from hook, hdc in next ch, dc in next ch, tr in next ch, dtr in next ch, skip next ch-6 loop, sc in next row-end sc] 6 times across to next corner, **ch 6, sc in 2nd ch from hook, hdc in next ch, dc in next ch, tr in next ch, dtr in next ch, skip next 4 sts, sc in next sc; rep from * across, omitting last, sc, join with a Sl st in first sc. Fasten off.

Finishing

Pin to measurements. Block.

Skill Level
Beginner

Yarn
Lion Brand LB Collection Cotton
Bamboo; 52% cotton, 48% bamboo; 245 yd (224 m)/3.5 oz (100
g): 1 skein each #139 Hibiscus (A)
and #174 Snapdragon (B)

DMC Pearl Cotton 8; 100% mercerized cotton; 95 yd (87 m/35 oz
(10 g); #712 off white (C): 1 ball

modern waves necklace

**Simple crochet techniques create a
unique necklace when the delicately
edged neckband is folded into place
with bobbles interspersed between.**

Designed by
Shelby Allaho

Hooks

1/B (2.25 mm), 2/C (2.75 mm), and 4/E (3.5mm)

Gauge

8 Fsc = 1" (2.5 cm)

Notions

Yarn needle

Rust-proof pins

Blocking board

Finished Size

14½" (36.8 cm) in length, measured down center of neckband

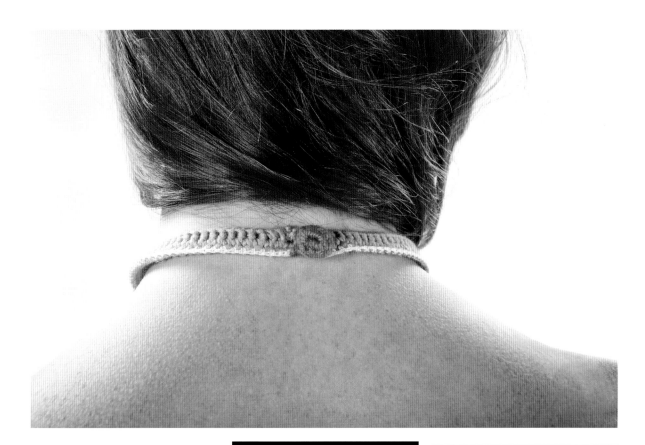

Special Stitches

Foundation single crochet (fsc): *Start with a slip knot, ch 2, insert hook in 2nd ch from hook, draw up a loop, yo, draw through 1 loop, yo, and draw through 2 loops – 1 single crochet with its own chain at bottom. Work next stitch under loops of that chain. Insert hook under 2 loops at bottom of the previous stitch, draw up a loop, yo and draw through 1 loop, yo and draw through 2 loops. Repeat for length of foundation.*

Necklace

Bobbles

(Make 6)

With hook 4/E (3.50 mm) hook and A, ch 2.

Rnd 1: Work 8 sc in second ch from hook, join with Sl st in first sc.

Rnds 2–3: Ch 1, sc in each sc around, join with Sl st in first sc.

Rnd 4: Ch 1, *sc in first sc, skip next sc; rep from * around, join with Sl st in first sc. Fasten off.

Neckband

With hook 2/C (2.75 mm) hook and B, work 380 Fsc or until foundation measures 54" (137 cm) long, turn.

Row 1 (RS): Ch 1, sc in each sc across, turn work to the right, (Sl st, ch 8, Sl st) in the middle of the end of the neckband for fastening loop. Fasten off.

Row 3: Change to hook size 1/B (2.25 mm), with RS facing, join C in first st of last row, ch 1, sc in each sc across. Fasten off.

Finishing

Weave in ends. Pin the neckband out straight to 55" (140 cm) in length on a blocking board, and wet or steam block. To make the waves in the neckband, place it on the template and follow the curves. Pin it into shape as you go, and insert the bobbles where indicated. With a half thickness of yarn B, stitch through the waves and bobbles to hold them in place, then, go back in the other direction to secure them. Remove pins. Stitch the remaining bobble to the end of the neckband opposite the fastening loop. Weave in ends. A final blocking is recommended.

Modern Waves Necklace Template

Skill Level

Easy

Yarn

Lion Brand LB Collection Cotton Bamboo; 52% cotton, 48% bamboo; 245 yd (224 m)/3.5 oz (100 g); Magnolia (A):1 skein

Katia Gatsby; 77% rayon, 15% nylon, 8% metallic polyester; 129 yd (118 m)/1.75 oz (50 g); #88504 Off White/Gold (B): 1 skein

circles in the sand neckpiece

Designed by
Shelby Allaho

This eye-catching neckpiece is created by crocheting four simple strips edged in metallic yarn, then stacking them and rolling the ends into scrolls. Try wearing it different ways and then when you decide your favorite, you can stitch Velcro where the scrolls touch to hold it in place. In a DK weight this piece makes a bold statement, try a finer weight yarn for a more delicate look.

Hooks	Gauge	Notions	Finished Size	
2/C (2.75 mm)	23 sts = 4" (10 cm)	Yarn needle	22" (56 cm) from scroll to scroll	**113**
1/B (2.25 mm)		Rust-proof pins		
		Piece of Velcro 1 1/8" x 3/8" (2.9 x 1 cm)		
		Sewing needle		
		Invisible nylon thread		

Special Stitches

Foundation single crochet (fsc): *Start with a slip knot, ch 2, insert hook in 2nd ch from hook, draw up a loop, yo, draw through 1 loop, yo, and draw through 2 loops—1 single crochet with its own chain at bottom. Work next stitch under loops of that chain. Insert hook under 2 loops at bottom of the previous stitch, draw up a loop, yo and draw through 1 loop, yo and draw through 2 loops. Repeat for length of foundation.*

Bands

Using larger hook and A, work 292 fsc for Band #1; work 289 fsc for Band #2; work 286 fsc for Band #3; and work 283 fsc for Band #4.

Band 1 = 44½" (113 cm) unblocked, and 47" (119 cm) blocked.

Band 2 = 44" (112 cm) unblocked, and 46½" (118 cm) blocked.

Band 3 = 43½" (110.5 cm) unblocked, and 46" (117 cm) blocked.

Band 4 = 43" (109 cm) unblocked, and 45½" (115.5 cm) blocked.

Rows 1–2: Ch 1, sc in back loop only of each st across, turn.

Row 3: Change smaller hook and B. Ch 1, sc in both loops of each st across. Fasten off.

Finishing

After completing all 4 bands, weave in all loose ends with a yarn needle. Pin out each band to required size on a blocking board, and wet or steam block.

Find the securing point on each band by folding them in half and marking the center. Then match them up. Band 1 will be on top with Bands 2, 3, and 4 underneath it in order, right sides and metallic edging facing up. Using a half thickness of B, invisibly stitch all four bands together at the securing point. Next stitch all of the bands together at each of the ends. Fold the joined ends approximately 1½" (3.8 cm) and then neatly roll up the bands in the direction of band 1 until the left scroll is 3 ⅛" (8 cm) in diameter and the right scroll is 3" (7.5 cm) in diameter (allowing the excess length in the bands to shift upwards). Pin scrolls in place. With a half thickness of yarn, invisibly stitch through each scroll to secure it from all sides.

Try on the neckpiece to determine how it is to be worn, and put pins in the scrolls to mark where the Velcro is to be positioned. Sew Velcro in place on the scrolls with invisible thread to hold the scrolls where you want them.

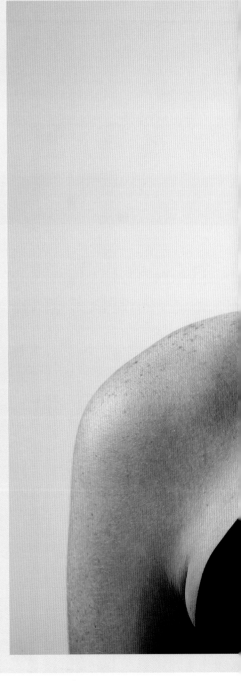

Skill Level

Intermediate

Yarn

Berroco Ultra Alpaca; 50% wool, 50% alpaca; 215 yd (198 m)/3.50oz (100 g): 1 skein each #6263 Carrots (A), #6275 Pea Soup Mix (B), #6253 Dijon (C), #6235 Fuchsia (D), and #6294 Turquoise Mix (E)

plaid wristlet purse

This fun purse was inspired by textile and jewelry elements, and the result is whimsical and elegant. Surface crochet is used to embellish the front flap and transform it into a plaid. Crochet bobble buttons fasten easily and are a unique closure. The chain wrist strap allows you to carry the purse hands free while looking fashionable.

Designed by
Shelby Allaho

Hooks

4/E (3.50 mm)

5/F (3.75 mm

10/J (6.00 mm)

Gauge

11 sts and 10 rows = 2" (5 cm) in front flap pattern

21 sts and 10 rows = 4" (10 cm) in back pattern.

Notions

Yarn needle

Rust-proof pins

Optional: Piece of cardboard 2" x 8½" (5 x 21.5 cm)

Two pieces of coordinating fabric 2½" x 9" (6.5 x 23 cm)

Invisible nylon thread

Finished Size

5 ¼" (14 cm) high x 9" (23 cm) wide, when closed (not including wrist chain)

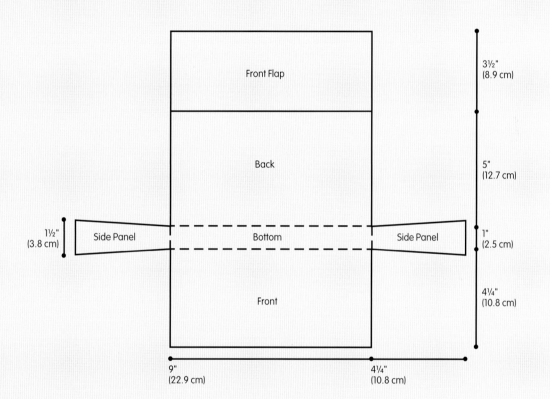

Special Stitches

Short single crochet (Sh sc): Insert hook in the horizontal bar underneath the front loop of st to be worked, yo, draw yarn though st, yo, draw yarn through 2 loops on hook.

Spike st: Insert hook in corresponding st 3 rows below, yo, draw yarn through st, yo, draw yarn through 2 loops on hook.

Invisible Fasten Off: Cut yarn leaving a 3" (7.5 cm) tail, yo and pull all the way through the work, as if to fasten off in the normal way, insert hook in both loops of 2nd st in rnd, yo and pull through, insert hook in front loop of last st in rnd, yo and pull down through.

To change color: Work the final yo of the sc of the old color, in the new color. Make sure that the old color is put to the wrong side of the front flap, after changing colors.

Front Flap

Starting at side edge, with 4/E (3.50 mm) hook and A, ch 9, change to B and ch 10.

Row 1 (WS): Working in the back bump on the underside of the ch, with B, sc in 2nd ch from hook, sc in next 8 ch, change to A, with A, sc in each remaining ch across, turn. (9 sc with B; 9 sc with A)

Row 2: With A, ch 1, sc in first 9 sts, change to B, with B, sc in each remaining sc across, turn. (9 sc with A; 9 sc with B)

Row 3: With B, ch 1, sc in first 9 sts, change to yarn A, sc in each remaining sc across, turn. (9 sc with B; 9 sc with A)

Rows 4–11: Rep Rows 2–3 (4 times), then rep row 2 once more. At end of last row, change to C, turn. Fasten off A and B. Turn.

Row 12: With C, ch 1, sc in first 9 sts, change to D, with D, sc in each remaining sc across, turn. (9 sc with D; 9 sc with C)

Row 13: With D, ch 1, sc in first 9 sts, change to C, with C, sc in each remaining st across, turn. (9 sc with C; 9 sc with D)

Rows 14–22: Rep Rows 12–13 (4 times), then rep rRow 12 once more. At end of last row, change to E, turn. Fasten off C and D.

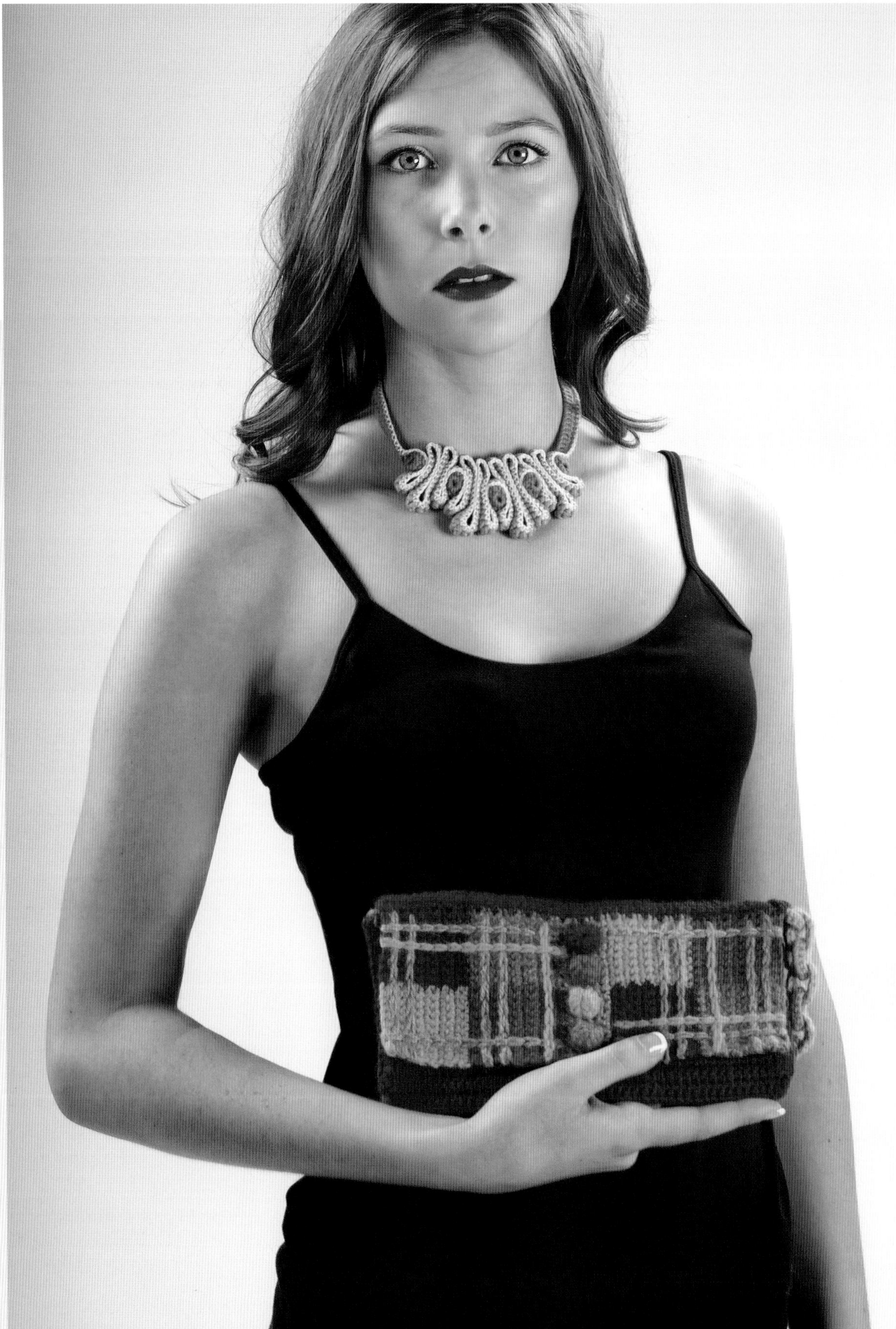

Rows 23–24: With E, ch 1, sc in each sc across, turn.

Row 25: Ch 1, sc in first 2 sts, *ch 2, skip next 2 st, sc in next 2 sts; rep from * across, turn.

Row 26: Ch 1, sc in first 2 sts, *2 sc in next ch-2 sp, sc in next 2 sts; rep from * across, turn.

Row 27: Rep Row 23, change to B.

Row 28: Rep Row 3.

Rows 29-38: Rep Rows 2–3 (5 times). At end of last row, change to C, turn. Fasten off A and B.

Row 39: Rep Row 13.

Rows 40-49: Rep Rows 12–13 (4 times). Fasten off.

Back

Row 1: With 4/E (3.50 mm) hook, join D in top right-hand corner of front flap, ch 1, sc in each row-end sc across, turn. (49 sts)

Row 2: Ch 1, sh sc in each st across, turn.

Row 3: Ch 1, sc in front loop of each st across, turn.

Row 4: Ch 1, sc in back loop of each st across, turn.

Rows 5–23: Rep rows 3–4 (9 times), then rep row 3 once more. Do not fasten off.

Bottom

Row 24: Ch 1, sh sc in each st across, turn.

Rows 25–29: Ch 1, sc in both loops each sc across, turn.

Row 30: Rep Row 24. Do not fasten off.

Front

Rows 31–50: Rep Rows 3–4 of back (10 times).

Row 51: Sl st in each st across. Fasten off.

Top Edging For Front of Purse

With 4/E (3.50 mm) hook, join B in the top right-hand corner of the front of purse, *spike sc 3 rows below**, ch 1, skip 1 st; rep from * across, ending last rep at **. Fasten off.

First Side Panel

Row 1: With 4/E (3.50 mm) hook, join A in last row-end st at end of row 24, ch 1, work sc in same row-end st, sc in each of next 6 row-end sts, turn. (7 sts)

Row 2: Ch 1, sh sc in each st across, turn.

Rows 3–24: Ch 1, sc in both loops of each st across, turn. Fasten off.

Second Side Panel

Row 1: With 4/E (3.50 mm) hook, join A in last row-end st at end of row 30, ch 1, work sc in same row-end st, sc in each of next 6 row-end sts, turn. (7 sts)

Rep Rows 2-24 of first side panel.

Primary Blocking

Neatly weave in all loose ends with a yarn needle. Pin the purse out flat on a blocking board, making sure to pin all edges straight. Wet or steam block. When purse is dry remove pins.

Surface Crochet Plaid Lines

Using 10/J (6.00 mm) hook, surface crochet in the holes created by the single crochet sts on the front flap, in the foll manner: insert hook in st in front flap keeping yarn under work: *yo, pull up a lp, skip a st, insert hook in next st; rep from * across as designated. Fasten off. Follow chart for placement of surface crochet of plaid lines.

With E, surface crochet from top to bottom edge of front flap in between rows: 2 and 3, 4 and 5, 13 and 14, 15 and 16, 34 and 35, 36 and 37, 46 and 47, 48 and 49. Then switch direction and surface crochet between the 2nd and 3rd sts from the ends of the rows at the top and bottom edges of the purse flap, beginning from the center of the purse to the edge on both sides.

With yarn C, surface crochet from top to bottom edge of front flap in between rows: 9 and 10, 29 and 30. Then switch direction and surface crochet between the 4th and 5th stitches from the top edge of the purse on the left side to the center of purse; and between the 4th and 5th sts from the bottom edge on the right side to the center of purse.

Side Panel Seams

Pin side panels to front and back of purse. With 5/F (3.75 mm) hook, and the side panel facing you, join D in bottom corner where side panel and back of purse meet, ch 1, sc in same st, *ch 1, working though double thickness of side and back, skip 1 row, sc in next row-end st; rep from * across to end of side panel. Fasten off. Work in the same manner for other side of panel, beg at the top of the purse and working down to the bottom matching sts. Seam second side panel in same manner.

Bobbles

(Make 1 each in A, B, C, and D)
With 5/F (3.75 mm) hook, ch 3.
Rnd 1: Work 9 dc in 3rd ch from hook, join with Sl st in first dc.
Rnd 2: *Skip next st, Sl st in next st; rep from * around to close up bobble. Fasten off.

Wrist Chain

With 5/F (3.75 mm) hook, ch 10, Sl st in back loop of first ch to form a ring.
Ring 1: Ch 1, work 12 sc in ring, join with Sl st in back loop of first sc. Work invisible fasten off.
Rings 2–11: Ch 10, insert ch in previous ring made, Sl st in back loop of first ch to form a ring, which links the 2 rings together, ch 1, work 12 sc in ring, join with Sl st in back loop of first sc. Work invisible fasten off.
Ring 12: Ch 10, insert ch in previous Ring made and in first ring made, sl st in back loop of first ch to form a ring, which links the 3 rings together, ch 1, work 12 sc in ring, join with Sl st in back loop of first sc. Work invisible fasten off. Weave in ends.

Tab for Wrist Chain

Row 1: With and 4/E (3.50 mm) hook and C, with RS of purse facing you, work surface crochet as follows: *insert hook in work from top to bottom, keep yarn under work, yo and pull up a lp* on edge of right hand corner of front flap, rep from * to * once on edge of right hand corner of front flap; rep from * to * on back of purse, turn. (3 sts)
Row 2: Ch 1, sc in each st across, turn. (3 sc)
Rows 3–4: Rep Row 2. Fasten off.

Finishing

Stitch bobbles to center front of purse, spacing them to match up with the spaces in the middle of the front flap. Fold the tab around one of the chains in the wrist chain, and sew end of tab to purse front flap and back. Weave in ends. For best results, block the purse again so that the folds in the side panels will be established.

An optional base can be made for the bottom of the purse. Placing right sides together, sew the fabric pieces together on 2 long sides and 1 short side. Turn right side out and insert cardboard. Fold edges of open end under. Invisibly sew end closed. Put the covered cardboard base inside the purse on the bottom. Tack it to the bottom of the purse by the corners and the middle of the long sides.

Front Flap Chart

Chart Key

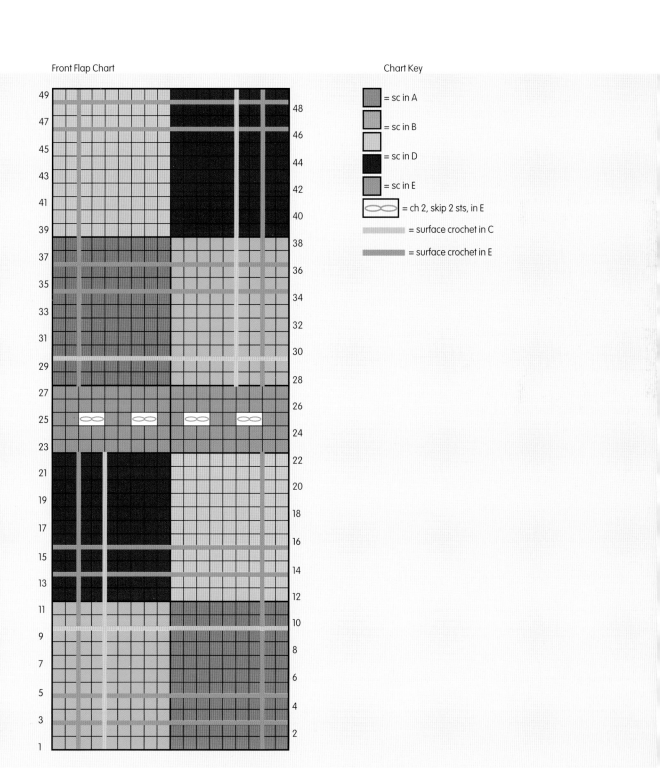

= sc in A

= sc in B

= sc in D

= sc in E

= ch 2, skip 2 sts, in E

= surface crochet in C

= surface crochet in E

Skill Level
Easy

Yarn
Louet Euroflax; 100% wet spin linen; 270 yds (246 m)/3.5 oz (100 g); #27 crabapple: 3 skeins

fabulous frills ruffle bag

Nothing makes a fashion statement like a lovely bag in a fabulous color. The linen yarn works up with a crisp feel and holds its shape. Embellished with ruffles and a touch of gold this bag is the perfect accessory for that special outfit.

Designed by
Margaret Hubert

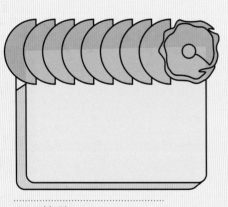

Assembly Diagram

Hook
5/F (3.75 mm)

Gauge
19 sts = 4" (10 cm) in pattern

Notions
Two 10 x 13" (25.5 x 33 cm) plastic canvas sheets

¾ yd (.7 m) polar fleece for inner lining to match

¾ yd (.7 m) silky lining fabric to match

Two Purse n-alize-it Handbag Handles

16" (40.5 cm) Chain Link Handle, item # 9020743, available at JoAnn Stores

One ¾" (2 cm) button

Yarn needle

Four yarn markers

Finished Size
14½" (37 cm) wide x 11" (28 cm) deep

123

Fabulous Frills
Ruffle Bag

Back/Front

(Make 2)

Ch 62.

Row 1: Sc in 4th ch from hook, *dc in next ch, sc in next ch; rep from * across, turn. (60 sts)

Row 2: Ch 3 (counts as a dc), skip first sc, *sc in next dc, dc in next sc; rep from * across, sc in top of turning ch, turn.

Rep Row 2 until piece measures 10" (25.5 cm) from beg. Fasten off.

Gusset

Ch 10.

Row 1: Sc in 4th ch from hook, *dc in next ch, sc in next ch; rep from * across, turn. (8 sts)

Rep Row 2 of back until piece measures 27" (68.5 cm). Fasten off.

Small Crescent Ruffles

(Make 8)

Ch 11.

Row 1: Sc in 2nd ch from hook and in each ch across, turn. (10 sc)

Row 2: Ch 3 (counts as dc here and throughout), skip first sc, 3 dc in each of next 8 sc, dc in last sc, turn. (26 dc)

Row 3: Ch 3, skip first dc, 3 dc in each of next 24 dc, dc in turning ch, turn. (74 dc)

Row 4: Ch 3, skip first dc, dc in each of the next 72 dc, dc in turning ch. Fasten off.

Large Rose

(Make one)

Ch 21.

Row 1: Sc in 2nd ch from hook and in each ch across, turn. (20 sc)

Row 2: Ch 3, skip first sc, 3 dc in next 18 sc, dc in last sc, turn. (56 dc)

Row 3: Ch 3, skip first dc, 2 dc in next 54 sts, dc in turning ch, turn. (110 dc)

Row 4: Ch 3, skip first dc, 2 tr in next 108 sts, dc in turning ch, turn. (218 tr)

Row 5: *Ch 3, skip next tr, sc in next tr; rep from * across. Fasten off.

Center for Large Rose

Ch 5, join with a Sl st to form a ring.

Rnd 1: Ch 1, 8 sc in ring, join with Sl st in first sc.

Rnd 2: Ch 1, 2 sc in each sc around, join with Sl st in first sc. (16 sc)

Rnd 3: Ch 1, sc in each sc around, join with Sl st in first sc. Fasten off, leaving an 18" (46 cm) sewing length. Sew center to center of large rose.

Twisted Cord

(Make 2)

Before beginning, cut 2 strands of yarn 10" (25.5 cm) long, set aside to be used to tie strands. Using 4 strands of yarn, each 96" (244 cm) long. Fold in half, anchoring the folded end, twist and twist these 2 strands until they become very tightly wound. Being sure not to let go of ends, bring both cut end and folded end together, hold up and allow to twist into a cord. Tie loose end tightly, about 1" (2.5 cm) from end. Weave each cord in and out of links of chain handle, bring ends back through one link and sew securely in place.

Before assembling bag line back, front and gusset as follows:

Cut polar fleece into two 10 x 13" (25.5 x 33 cm) pieces, pin in place on back and front, sew in place. Cut one piece 1 x 27" (2.5 x 68.5 cm), pin in place on gusset, sew into place.

Finishing

Before completing lining, sew small crescent ruffles and large rose into place attaching to crocheted fabric and polar fleece lining for stability. Starting at top left-hand corner of front of bag, sewing one crescent at a time, pin into place, leaving the last row of each crescent to extend over the top of bag, and placing each crescent to overlap the previous one, ending with the large rose at top right corner.

Cut 2 pieces of silky lining fabric 11 x 14" (218 x35.5 cm) for back and front, cut one piece 2 x 28" (5 x 71 cm) for gusset. Fold edges to wrong side ½" (13 mm). Pin lining to back and front. Sew sides and top, before sewing bottom edge, slide 1 piece of plastic canvas between the polar fleece and the lining fabric, complete sewing bottom edge closed. Fold edges of lining fabric to wrong side ½" (13 mm). Pin lining to gusset and sew all around. When all pieces are lined, place a marker 3" (7.5 cm) down from top of bag on both sides of back and front. With right sides together, pin gusset into place. Sew into place, starting at first marker, down side, across bottom and up to second marker.

Edging

With RS of bag facing, join a double strand of yarn in top right-hand corner of back, ch 1, work sc in each of 60 sts across top of back, 3 sc in corner, 9 sc down slit to top of gusset, skip 1 st, sc in next 3 sts at top of gusset, skip 1 st, work 9 sc on other side of slit, 3 sc in corner, sc in each of next 30 sts, ch 10 (button loop), sc in each of next 30 sts, join with Sl st in first sc. Fasten off.

Sew button on back, attach chain link handles to top corners of back and front.

abbreviations and symbols

Abbreviations

Here is the list of standard abbreviations used for crochet.

approx	approximately
beg	begin/beginning
bet	between
BL	back loop(s)
bo	bobble
BP	back post
BPdc	back post double crochet
BPsc	back post single crochet
BPtr	back post triple crochet
CC	contrasting color
ch	chain
ch-	refers to chain or space previously made, e.g., ch-1 space
ch lp	chain loop
ch-sp	chain space
CL	cluster(s)
cm	centimeter(s)
cont	continue
dc	double crochet
dc2tog	double crochet 2 stitches together
dec	decrease/decreases/ decreasing
dtr	double treble
FL	front loop(s)
foll	follow/follows/following
FP	front post
FPdc	front post double crochet
FPsc	front post single crochet
FPtr	front post triple crochet
g	gram(s)
hdc	half double crochet
inc	increase/increases/increasing
lp(s)	loop(s)
Lsc	long single crochet
m	meter(s)
MC	main color
mm	millimeter(s)

oz	ounce(s)
p	picot
patt	pattern
pc	popcorn
pm	place marker
prev	previous
qutr	quadruple triple crochet
rem	remain/remaining
rep	repeat(s)
rev sc	reverse single crochet
rnd(s)	round(s)
RS	right side(s)
sc	single crochet
sc2tog	single crochet 2 stitches together
sk	skip
Sl st	slip stitch
sp(s)	space(s)
st(s)	stitch(es)
tbl	through back loop(s)
tch	turning chain
tfl	through front loop(s)
tog	together
tr	triple crochet
trtr	triple treble crochet
tr2tog	triple crochet 2 together
TS	T unisian simple stitch
WS	wrong side(s)
yd	yard(s)
yo	yarn over
yoh	yarn over hook
[ ]	Work instructions within brackets as many times as directed
*	Repeat instructions following the single asterisk as directed
* *	Repeat instructions between asterisks as many times as directed or repeat from a given set of instructions

Term Conversions

Crochet techniques are the same universally, and everyone uses the same terms. However, US patterns and UK patterns are different because the terms denote different stitches. Here is a conversion chart to explain the differences.

US	UK
single crochet (sc)	double crochet (dc)
half double crochet (hdc)	half treble (htr)
double crochet (dc)	treble (tr)
triple crochet (tr)	double treble (dtr)

Stitch Key

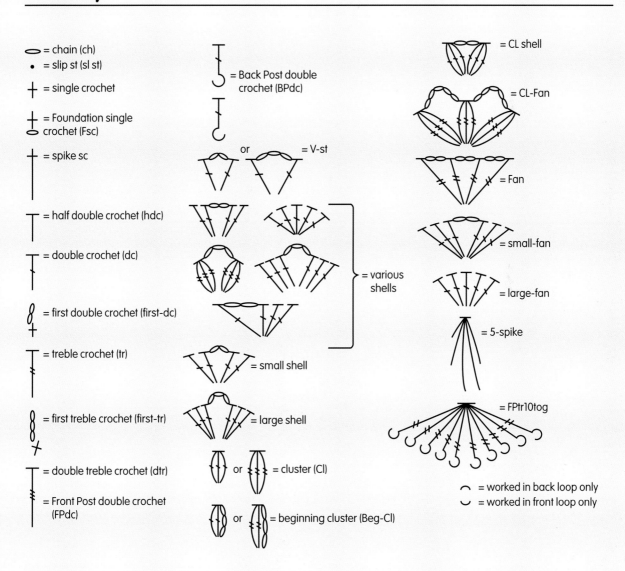

○ = chain (ch)

• = slip st (sl st)

+ = single crochet

+ = Foundation single crochet (Fsc)

+ = spike sc

T = half double crochet (hdc)

T = double crochet (dc)

δ = first double crochet (first-dc)

T = treble crochet (tr)

δ = first treble crochet (first-tr)

T = double treble crochet (dtr)

= Front Post double crochet (FPdc)

= Back Post double crochet (BPdc)

or = V-st

= various shells

= small shell

= large shell

or = cluster (Cl)

or = beginning cluster (Beg-Cl)

= CL shell

= CL-Fan

= Fan

= small-fan

= large-fan

= 5-spike

= FPtr10tog

⌢ = worked in back loop only

⌣ = worked in front loop only

about
the author

Margaret Hubert of Pawling, New York, is the author of more than 20 crochet and knitting books, including *Plus Size Crochet, Knits for Men, Knit or Crochet—Have It Your Way, The Complete Photo Guide to Crochet, The Complete Photo Guide to Knitting, The Granny Square Book,* and *Lacework for Adventurous Crocheters.* She has enjoyed a lifelong career designing both crochet and knit patterns for yarn companies and book and magazine publishers. Margaret also teaches at yarn shops, retreats, and national gatherings, and rarely misses a national conference in the needle arts field. A word traveler, Margaret pays close attention to the fashions in Europe and spots trends as they hit New York. In 2012, Margaret was inducted into the Jean Leinhauser Crochet Hall of Fame. Follow Margaret's blog:
http://margaretshooksandneedles.
blogspot.com/

Acknowledgments

There are many people I would like to thank for helping me put this book together.

I want to thank Linda Neubauer, my editor, for all the help and support that she constantly gives to me. I have said it before, but I'll say it again, without Linda, there would be no book. Thank you also to the editorial, design, and production staff at Creative Publishing international.

My deepest appreciation goes to the guest designers who contributed their fabulous designs: Shelby Allaho, Doris Chan, Ellen Gormley, Sharon Hubert Valencia, Tatyana Mirer, and Shannon Mullett-Bowlsby.

The many yarn companies who donate yarn for the projects deserve a huge thank you. They include Art Yarn, Aunt Lydia's Yarn, Berroco Yarn, Bijou Basin Yarns, Blue Heron Yarns, Blue Sky Alpacas, Cascade Yarn, Classic Elite Yarn, Handmaiden Yarn, Lion Brand Yarn, Lorna's Laces, Louet Yarn, Louisa Harding Yarn, Lucci Yarn, Malabrigo Yarn, Patons Yarn, Plymouth Yarn, and Tahki/Stacey Charles Yarn.

I'd also like to thank all the people behind the scenes who help put a book together, especially K. J. Hay and Karen Manthey, technical editors. Jeannine Buehler, Paula Alexander, and Nancy Smith helped me to crochet some of the projects in the book. Frances Feery helps me to proofread.

Many thanks to all.

about
the designers

Shelby Allaho

Shelby has won numerous design awards, and her work has been published in *Interweave Crochet* and *Inside Crochet*, as well as in books from Sixth and Spring Books, and Sterling Publishing. She specializes in designing unique accessories for women and children, in traditional and freeform crochet. You can follow Shelby on her blog at www.stitch-story.com

Doris Chan

Doris has designed hundreds of garments and accessories for yarn companies, magazines and books and has written articles and essays about crochet technique. Her books, *Amazing Crochet Lace* (Potter Craft, 2006) and *Everyday Crochet* (Potter Craft, 2007), the award-wining *Crochet Lace Innovations* (Potter Craft, 2010) and *Convertible Crochet* (Potter Craft, coming in May 2013) were wonderful opportunities for her to explore and share her crochet ideas, occasional angst and her modus operandi of top-down, seamless construction. Doris is an avid professional member of the Crochet Guild of America and writes a popular, award-winning blog at http://dorischancrochet.com.

Ellen

Ellen stitched more than 80 afghans before beginning her design career in 2004. Now, Ellen has sold more than 200 designs, and been published numerous times in many crochet magazines including *Interweave Crochet*, *Crochet Today*, *Crochet!*, *Crochet World,* and *Inside Crochet*. Ellen is a crochet expert on the PBS show *Knit and Crochet Now!* She also teaches online crochet classes for anniescatalog.com. Her two books are *Go Crochet! Afghan Design Workbook* and *Learn Bruges Lace*.
You can follow Ellen on her blog at www.GoCrochet.com and as 'GoCrochet' on Twitter and www.Ravelry.com.

Tatyana Mirer

Tatyana is a knitwear and crochet designer and teacher. Her crochet works have been published in various magazines and books including *Crochet Master Class, The Complete Photo Guide To Crochet, Crochet Today, Crochet!, Family Circle Easy Crochet Book*. Tatyana teaches at yarn shops, guilds, and retreats. Her professional background is in fashion design. She likes to use a variety of crochet techniques and apply them to garments for figure-flattering fashion.

Shannon Mullett-Bowlsby

Shannon is the co-founder of The Shibaguyz and Shibaguyz Designz. Shannon is an award-winning designer, skilled in both crochet and knit, having published numerous patterns for magazines, yarn companies, and the Shibaguyz pattern line. He currently has five of his own books published with another scheduled for release later this year. A skilled instructor, Shannon's classes are often sold out and are always highly recommended by his students.
Jason Mullett-Bowlsby, photographer for this book, is the other co-founder of The Shibaguyz. Jason's skills in photography, graphic design, and layout can be seen in many of their clients pattern lines as well as in The Shibaguyz' own pattern book, *Urban Edge*.

Sharon Hubert Valencia

Sharon's designing career began at a very young age while sitting in her mother's knit shop. Surrounded by a variety of fibers, she was inspired to make doll clothes and baby sweaters--projects she could complete in a short period of time. Her first design was published while still in high school and this encouraged her to attend Fashion Institute of Technology and pursue a career in fashion design. While she enjoyed studying at FIT, she didn't see fashion design as a strong career path for her so she transferred to study medicine and is currently a podiatrist in private practice. Recently, her mother, Margaret Hubert, petitioned her to submit a design for her book *The Granny Square Book*. This project rekindled her interest in designing so she submitted a few designs to magazines and made the cover of *Crochet! Magazine*.

don't miss these other books by margaret hubert

Available online or at your
local craft or book store.

Plus Size Crochet
9781589233393

Knit or Crochet—
Have It Your Way
97815892343314

The Granny Square Book
9781589236387

The Complete Photo
Guide to Crochet
9781589234727

The Complete Photo
Guide to Knitting
9781589235423

Lacework for Adventurous
Crocheters
9781589237346

**Creative Publishing
international**

www.CreativePub.com

Our books are available as E-Books, too!

Many of our bestselling titles are now available as E-Books. Visit www.Qbookshop.com to find
links to e-vendors!